TRADITIONAL LOGIC

Advanced Formal Logic

━ BOOK II ━

By Martin Cothran

CLASSICAL TRIVIUM CORE SERIES

Traditional Logic: Book II
Advanced Formal Logic
Copyright © 2000 Memoria Press
ISBN: 1-930953-12-7

4103 Bishop Lane, Louisville, Kentucky 40218
www.memoriapress.com

Table of Contents

To the Teacher

The two books together constitute a complete course in formal logic at the junior and senior high school levels.

_____ **What This Book Covers.** This book is a continuation of *Traditional Logic, Book I: An Introduction to Formal Logic*, and presupposes a knowledge of the material in that book. The two books together constitute a complete course in formal logic at the junior and senior high school levels.

Book I covers the three acts of the mind involved in logic: simple apprehension, judgement and deductive inference. In this book, we continue the study of deductive inference with the treatment of figure and mood in simple syllogisms, complex syllogisms and hypothetical reasoning. We also have one chapter on the oblique syllogism, which is a variant of the traditional categorical syllogism.

Like the first book, daily exercise sets are given at the end of each chapter to ensure comprehension and mastery of the material at every level. It has always seemed to me that logic instruction books are plagued by one or both of two problems: they are either too difficult for use at the high school level, or they are so simplified and cursory in their treatment that they do not constitute a truly comprehensive and rigorous course in the subject. The structure of the exercises in this book is meant to remedy both problems by guiding the student through sometimes difficult material in such a way as to make the learning of it as simple and straightforward as the subject itself allows. If I have done my job right, then whatever difficulties encountered will not be because of poor presentation, but because of the inherent complexity of the material.

One marked difference between this and the first book is the inclusion of more "real life" contemporary examples of arguments in the exercises. I intentionally avoided them in *Book I* because I wanted the student to concentrate on the form of arguments to the exclusion of all else. We continue the study of form in this book, of course, but the student should be more prepared at this point in his understanding of logic to accommodate a wide variety and complexity of content. The examples in the chapters themselves continue to concentrate on simple examples, most of them theological or philosophical in content. But, beginning in chapter 6, the student is introduced to examples that have political and social relevance.

Several additional features differentiate this from the earlier book, including writing assignments at the end of each chapter and case studies in the later chapters of the book. The writing assignments are optional, of course, but they provide an excellent way to integrate logic, history, philosophy, religion and writing. The case studies show the relevance and importance of logic in history, literature, religion and philosophy. These are some of the notable examples of how the argument forms covered in this book have been used by the great thinkers of the Western world to deal with issues that many times transcend the time and circumstance in which they were uttered. They are meant to inspire the individual teacher to find such examples himself. In fact, the good teacher will collect many more as his years of experience in teaching logic grows.

_____ **Whom This Book is For.** Both this and the previous book were written with junior high and senior high students in mind. The first book is meant to easily accommodate 7th and 8th graders. These students, however, will find this book more difficult going than the first. It is not, however, out of the reach of exceptional 7th and 8th graders, although it is probably best suited for use at about the 9th grade. Students with training in classical subjects such as Latin will be the best prepared for this logic program.

_____ **Some Suggestions on Using This Book.** I would like to make several suggestions to both the home schooling parents and the classroom teachers who use this book. The first has to do with challenges posed by the presentation of more difficult material.

Because of the level of difficulty *Book II* will take relatively longer than *Book I*. Families and schools using the book over the course of one year will probably want to finish *Book I* before the end of the first semester to allow several extra weeks to cover the material in *Book II*. Those that have used a semester to cover *Book I* might consider skipping one or two chapters in the books (Chapter 4 in *Book II*, for example, is not essential to the subsequent material.) Either book, of course, could be used as the basis for year-long rather than a one-semester course.

_____ **Suggestions on Classroom Discussion.** My own classroom experience has convinced me that nothing gets a student's attention more than the discussion of thorny religious, philosophical and social issues. I never plan for these in my own classroom presentation, partly because I teach in a cottage school environment where I only have one hour a week with the students, and partly because of my own teaching style. These issues do seem to come up on a regular basis—either from a student who has seen or heard something relevant that interests him, or from me, when I have heard something on the radio or read something in the newspaper that exemplifies some form of argument we have studied.

The case studies show the relevance and importance of logic in history, literature, religion and philosophy.

It will always be the teacher and the student who will find the most relevant topics for discussion.

Although the case studies are meant, in part, to engender some of this kind of discussion, the most relevant topics cannot be included in this book, since the shelf life of most relevant issues, particularly political and social issues, is very short. That is, of course, the problem with trying to be relevant: One becomes irrelevant rather quickly.

While we have included many examples in this book that are standard topics in many Christian and home schools, it will always be the teacher and the students who will find the most relevant topics for discussion. Simply reading the daily newspaper and listening to the news will yield a treasure trove of argument forms (valid and invalid) for profitable classroom discussion. In this age of symbolic media such as television, which dulls the rational faculties, the teacher will have done the student a favor if, during the course of the class, he (the student) acquires the habit of analyzing everything he sees, hears and reads.

One excellent way to foster interest in the subject of logic is to arrange to have the students all read the same material outside of class. Having them all read a particular columnist in the local newspaper or in a magazine (Christian families and schools might consider sources such as *World* magazine) would be an excellent way to provide a common fund of material to facilitate discussion and to engender competition in identifying arguments.

When a classroom discussion builds a head of steam, and students begin to address one another, I have found that the teacher can calmly retreat to the board and begin writing down the arguments being expressed by the most vigorous proponents of each position. It doesn't take the students long to realize that the logical skeleton of their arguments has been set down in very clear terms. Sometimes they like what they see, but more often they are forced to qualify their statements and sometimes take them back. In either case, they have been forced to logically analyze what they have said. These situations make for very teachable moments.

The teacher will notice that there are many exercises in this book that require the student to construct arguments of the form being studied. These exercises are extremely important, since they force the student to analyze the structure of the argument form he is studying. These exercises are also useful in the classroom. Teachers might, for example, with a few minutes left in class, ask students to create a syllogism in whatever argument form they are studying. As soon as they have done it correctly (and no sooner), they can be dismissed. I have used this technique to great benefit.

_____ **Traditional Logic vs. Modern Logic.** I would also like to say something about the relationship between traditional and modern symbolic logic, since I anticipate questions from some about material covered in other programs that is not covered here. Truth tables, for example, and other features of the calculus of modern logic are things I have chosen not to cover in this program in favor of a more traditional approach to the subject. There are several reasons for this.

Traditional logic is based on metaphysical realism; in its emphasis on terms and their relationships, it assumes that terms stand for concepts and concepts for real essences. In other words, in the perennial debate over how we can know anything, traditional logic very plainly assumes that things are and that we can know them as they are. Modern logic, on the other hand, assumes a sort of metaphysical nominalism; that is, the idea that terms are merely labels, invented for our convenience, but not necessarily signifying anything real.

This creates problems too technical to delve into here. Suffice it to say that this book is based on the older and more philosophically sound approach which is, in my opinion, much more closely in accord with the Christian worldview. That is not to say that I think a study of modern logic is not profitable. I do believe, however, that a student will profit more from it if he already has a solid grounding in a system with correct assumptions.

_____ **Acknowledgments.** The material for this book was based on a number of important sources. Among the most important are: *Formal Logic*, by Jacques Maritain; *Basic Logic*, by Raymond McCall; and perhaps the most helpful book I have come across on the subject of logic, *Introduction to Logic*, by Andrew H. Bachhuber, S. J. I have tried not to directly lift anything from these books, although a few examples will seem extremely familiar to anyone who has read these books. I have also used the same breakdown for translating ordinary language arguments that is used in *Philosophy Made Simple*, by Richard H. Popkin and Avrum Stroll, a book that contains one of the best short presentations of traditional logic available.

I would also like to thank the students in my logic classes over the past years for their help in pointing out mistakes in the class notes which formed the basis for this book. I would like particularly to thank Ruth John, one of my veteran students who helped proof the book. But it is Cheryl Lowe of Memoria Press who, with the exception of myself, has spent more time than anyone else on the book.

But despite the many hours Cheryl has spent finding my errors, there are undoubtedly a few we missed. Anyone finding mistakes in the book is welcome (and encouraged) to bring them to our attention. I would also urge parents and teachers using this book to share their suggestions for teaching the material. Both of these things can be done by visiting our website at: www.memoriapress.com. We will try to incorporate all of your suggestions in some way, either in a future revision of the book or through online helps.

Training in logic will provide a student with a lifelong habit of mind which he will take with him into every activity in his life that involves thought—which is to say, every activity. Not everyone becomes a scientist, or accountant, or teacher, but everyone has to think. And there is no better way to prepare for this universal occupation than the study of logic.

Martin Cothran

> **T**his book is based on the older and more philosophically sound approach which is, in my opinion, much more closely in accord with the Christian worldview.

> "Logic is the anatomy of thought."
>
> **—John Locke**

Figure in Syllogisms

_____ **Introduction.** Now that we have mastered the rules of validity for categorical syllogisms, we turn to figures and moods. Categorizing syllogisms according to figure and mood will deepen our understanding of the syllogism and give us a short cut in determining validity.

The *figure* of the syllogism can be defined as follows:

The figure of a syllogism is the disposition (or location) of terms in the premises.

The figure of a syllogism is determined by the position of the middle term. There are four figures in all.

_____ **Review of Terms.** In order to properly understand syllogistic figures, we must remember the terms in a syllogism and the letters that designate them. We must remember that the letter **P** designates the major term (which is the predicate of the conclusion). The letter **S** designates the minor term (which is the subject of the conclusion); and the letter **M** designates the middle term (which is the term that appears in both premises, but not in the conclusion).

We must also remember that the premise that contains the major term (which we call the major premise) always comes first. Thus, a typical syllogism might look like this:

All M is P
All S is M
Therefore, all S is P

The location of **M** (the middle term) in each premise will tell us what figure the syllogism is in.

_____ **The First Figure.** In a syllogism of the First Figure, the middle term is the subject in the major premise and the predicate in the minor premise. We call this figure *sub-prae*, which is short for

The figure of a syllogism is the disposition (or location) of terms in the premises.

subjectum-**prae**dicatum, which is Latin for **subject-predicate**—the subject being the place of the middle term in the major premise and predicate being the place of the middle term in the minor premise.

An example of a **sub-prae** or **First Figure** syllogism would be:

All human beings^M are mortal^P
All boys^S are human beings^M
Therefore, all boys^S are mortal^P

We must also remember that the major premise is always put first in a syllogism.

*Sub-prae*_____

You can see that the middle term is the subject in the major premise and the predicate in the minor premise. Therefore, it is *sub-prae*.

_____ **The Second Figure.** In a syllogism of the **Second Figure**, the middle term is the predicate in the major premise and the predicate in the minor premise.

We term this figure **prae-prae**, which is short for **prae**dicatum-**prae**dicatum, which is Latin for **predicate-predicate**, the predicate being the place of the middle term in both premises.

An example of a **prae-prae** or **Second Figure** syllogism would be:

All men^P are mortal^M
No angels^S are mortal^M

Therefore, no angels^S are men^P

*Prae-prae*_____

P　　　(M)
S　　　(M)
S　　　P

You can see that the middle term is the predicate in both the major and minor premises of this argument. Therefore, this syllogism is *prae-prae*.

_____ **The Third Figure.** In a syllogism of the **Third Figure**, the middle term is the subject in the major premise and also the subject in the minor premise:

We term this figure **sub-sub**, which is short for **sub**jectum-**sub**jectum, the subject being the place of the middle term in both premises.

An example of a **sub-sub** or **Third Figure** syllogism would be:

All human beings^M are mortal^P
Some human beings^M are boys^S

Therefore, some boys^S are mortal^P

*Sub-sub*_____

Here the middle term is the subject in both the major and minor premises of the argument. Therefore, this syllogism is *sub-sub*.

_____ **The Fourth Figure (Indirect First).** There is also what some have called a **Fourth Figure**. However, **Fourth Figure** syllogisms are actually just another form of the First. They are what we will call the **Indirect First**.

In a **Fourth Figure** syllogism, the middle term is the predicate in the major premise and the subject in the minor premise. In other words, a **prae-sub**. We say it is not a figure in and of itself but only a form of the First because the only difference between it and the First is in the grammar of the syllogism; the arrangement of the words only makes it look different, but logically it is the same.

An example of the **Fourth Figure** would be:

All Romans^P are men^M
All men^M are mortal^S
Therefore, some mortals^S are Romans^P

As you can see, the middle term (**men**) is the predicate in the major premise and the subject in the minor premise.

Prae-sub_____

This Fourth Figure is sometimes called the **Galenic** figure because it was Claudius Galen, who lived from 131 A. D. to about 200 A. D., who first considered that it was a separate figure. Galen was considered the chief authority on medicine for over a thousand years. But while Galen and many modern logicians think the Fourth Figure is distinct from the First, Aristotle and all the rest of the ancient logicians thought it was only another form of the First.

We will side with the ancients and concentrate primarily on the first three figures. However, we do encounter syllogisms in this form, so we need to be prepared to handle them.

_____ **How to Remember the Figures.** There are many Latin sayings that logicians in the Middle Ages invented to help us to remember certain things in logic. The Latin saying that helps us to remember figures goes like this:

Sub-prae prima, bis prae secunda, tertia sub bis.

It means, **Sub-prae first, prae twice second, sub twice third**. In other words, **sub-prae** is the First Figure, **prae-prae** (**prae twice**) is the Second, and **sub-sub** (**sub twice**) is the Third. By memorizing this saying, you will be able to remember where the middle term is in each of the three figures.

_____ **Summary.** This chapter concerns the **figure** of syllogisms. The figure of a syllogism is defined as **the disposition of terms in the premises**. The terms in a syllogism can be arranged in one of three (some would say four) different ways. We identify the figures

While Galen and many modern logicians think the Fourth Figure is distinct from the First, Aristotle and all the rest of the ancient logicians thought it was only another form of the First.

according to the location of the middle term.

A syllogism in which the middle term is the subject in the major premise and the predicate in the minor premise is called a ***sub-prae*** or ***First Figure*** syllogism. A syllogism in which the middle term is the predicate in the major premise and the predicate in the minor premise is called a ***prae-prae*** or ***Second Figure*** syllogism. A syllogism in which the middle term is the subject in the major premise and the subject in the minor premise is called a ***sub-sub*** or ***Third Figure*** syllogism.

There is also an ***Indirect First Figure***, which some logicians have considered to be another figure altogether—a ***Fourth Figure*** syllogism. Its middle term appears in the predicate of the major premise and in the subject of the minor premise, making it a ***prae-sub***. But it only looks like a different figure and is really just a form of the First.

We identify the figures according to the location of the middle term.

_____ **Exercises for Day 1.** **Peruse entire chapter. Then read the introductory section at the very beginning of chapter 1. Read this section carefully and try to understand it as best you can.**

1. What are we discussing in this chapter?

2. Explain what the word *figure* means as used in this chapter.

3. How many figures are there?

4. What is *disposition*?

Read section titled, "The First Figure." Read it carefully.

5. What is the Latin term for a syllogism in the First Figure?

6. How do we know a syllogism is in the First Figure?

7. Fill in the following chart:

> **First Figure (*sub-prae*)**
>
> M is the _____ (subject or predicate) in the *major* premise
> M is the _____ (subject or predicate) in the *minor* premise

8. Show, using the symbols S, P and M, how a *sub-prae* syllogism is constructed.

9. Construct a *sub-prae* syllogism using different terms than the ones in the text.

_____ **Exercises for Day 2.** **Read section titled, "The Second Figure." Read the entire section carefully.**

10. What is the Latin term for a syllogism in the Second Figure?

11. How do we know a syllogism is in the Second Figure?

12. Fill in the following chart:

> **Second Figure (*prae-prae*)**
>
> M is the _____ in the *major* premise
> M is the _____ in the *minor* premise

13. Show, using the symbols S, P and M, how a *prae-prae* syllogism is constructed.

14. Construct a *prae-prae* syllogism using different terms than the ones in the text.

Read section titled, "The Third Figure." Read it carefully.

15. What is the Latin term for a syllogism in the Third Figure?

16. How do we know a syllogism is in the Third Figure?

17. Fill in the following chart:

> **Third Figure (*sub-sub*)**
>
> M is the _____ in the *major* premise
>
> M is the _____ in the *minor* premise

18. Show, using the symbols S, P and M, how a *sub-sub* syllogism is constructed.

19. Construct a *sub-sub* syllogism using different terms than the ones in the text.

_____ **Exercises for Day 3.** **Read section titled "The Fourth Figure (Indirect First)." Read the entire section carefully.**

20. What is the Latin term for a syllogism in the Fourth Figure?

21. How do we know a syllogism is in the Fourth Figure?

22. Fill in the following chart:

> **Fourth Figure-Indirect First (*prae-sub*)**
>
> M is: _____   in the   *major* premise
>
> M is: _____   in the   *minor* premise

23. Show, using the symbols S, P and M, how a *prae-sub* syllogism is constructed.

24. Construct a *prae-sub* syllogism using different terms than the ones in the text.

25. Fourth Figure syllogisms are just another form of what?

26. What is the Fourth Figure sometimes called?

Read section titled, "How to Remember the Figures."

27. What is the Latin saying invented to help remember the figures?

28. What does this saying mean?

_____ **Exercises for Day 4.**

29. Identify the terms, identify the position of the middle term and determine the figure of each syllogism:

No liberals are conservatives
Allen is a conservative
Therefore, Allen is not a liberal

        S: _____
        P: _____
        M: _____

M= _____ (*sub* or *prae*)
M= _____ (*sub* or *prae*)

■ First ■ Second ■ Third ■ Fourth

All Democrats are big spenders
President Clinton is a Democrat
Therefore, President Clinton is a big spender

        S: _____
        P: _____
        M: _____

M= _____
M= _____

■ First ■ Second ■ Third ■ Fourth

Some men are physicists
All physicists are brilliant
Therefore, some brilliant things are men

        S: _____
        P: _____
        M: _____

M= _____
M= _____

■ First ■ Second ■ Third ■ Fourth

No beggars can be choosers
That man is a beggar
Therefore, that man cannot be a chooser

        S: _____
        P: _____
        M: _____

M= _____
M= _____

■ First ■ Second ■ Third ■ Fourth

No men are gods
All men are mortal
Therefore, some mortals are not gods

        S: _____
        P: _____
        M: _____

M= _____
M= _____

■ First ■ Second ■ Third ■ Fourth

30. Complete the following diagram by giving the form of each statement and showing whether each term is distributed or undistributed. [Review]

DISTRIBUTION

Letter designation	Form (e.g. "All S is P")	Subject-Term	Predicate-Term
A	_____	_____	_____
I	_____	_____	_____
E	_____	_____	_____
O	_____	_____	_____

31. Indicate which figures the following syllogisms are in:

All dogs bark ■ First ■ Second ■ Third ■ Fourth
Rover is a dog
Therefore, Rover barks

All bees sting ■ First ■ Second ■ Third ■ Fourth
All stinging things should be avoided
Therefore, bees should be avoided.

No horse can fly ■ First ■ Second ■ Third ■ Fourth
Pegasus is a horse
Therefore, Pegasus cannot fly

All music is of some value ■ First ■ Second ■ Third ■ Fourth
Some music is classical music
Therefore, some classical music is of some value

32. Think up your own syllogism for each of the four figures.

Read section titled, "Summary." Read it carefully.

33. Tell whether the following are true or false:

T F We label a First Figure syllogism *sub-prae*.
T F The Third Figure is really just a form of the First Figure.
T F *Prae-prae* is short for the Latin *praedicatum-praedicatum*.
T F In a syllogism of the Second Figure, the major term is the subject in the major premise and the predicate of the minor premise.
T F The figure of a syllogism is the disposition of terms in the conclusion.
T F The Fourth Figure is sometimes called the Galenic figure.

"Logic takes care of itself; all we have to do is to look and see how it does it."

—**Ludwig Wittgenstein**

Mood in Syllogisms

_____ **Introduction.** In the last chapter, we discussed the four ways a syllogism can be formed according to the disposition of terms. These four ways we called a syllogism's *figure*. In this chapter, we will talk about *mood*.

We defined *figure* as the *disposition* (or *location*) of terms in a syllogism—In other words, how the *terms* are arrayed in the syllogism. *Mood* is defined as follows:

Mood is the disposition of the premises according to quantity and quality.

For example, we say that a syllogism has the mood **AA** when the first (or *major*) premise is an A statement and the second (or *minor*) premise is also an A statement. Again we say that a syllogism has the mood **EA** when the first premise is an E statement and the second premise is an A statement.

Look at the following syllogism:

> All mortals must die
> All men are mortal
> Therefore, all men must die

In what mood is this syllogism? We see that the first premise is an A statement, and the second is an A statement. Therefore, the mood of the syllogism is **AA**.

Let's take another example:

> No men are immortal
> All angels are immortal
> Therefore, no angels are men

What mood is this syllogism in? We see that the first premise is an E statement. The second is an A statement. Therefore, the mood of the syllogism is EA.

> **T**he mood of a syllogism is the disposition of the premises according to quantity and quality.

Be careful that your premises are in the proper place— major premise first and minor premise second. If they are not in the proper order, you can easily misidentify the mood of a syllogism.

Since there are four different kinds of statements (A, E, I and O), they can be combined into 16 different moods (4 x 4) as follows:

MAJOR

	A	**E**	**I**	**O**
A	AA	EA	IA	OA
E	AE	EE	IE	OE
I	AI	EI	II	OI
O	AO	EO	IO	OO

MINOR

Be careful that your premises are in the proper place—major premise first and minor premise second. If they are not in the proper order, you can easily misidentify the mood of a syllogism.

_____ **Figure and Mood.** Furthermore, each of these sixteen moods can be found in each of the four figures. In other words, a syllogism in the First Figure can be in the mood AA, AE, AI, AO, EA, EO, etc. This means that there are a total of 64 different kinds of syllogisms according to mood and figure (16 moods x 4 figures).

But although there are 64 different kinds of syllogisms, not all of them are valid. In some cases, whole moods are invalid. For example, EE syllogisms, whether they are in the First, Second, Third or Fourth figure are invalid. Why? Remember Rule V in chapter 13 of Book I? It said that no conclusion can follow from two negative premises. E is a negative statement, therefore, a syllogism in which both premises are E statements cannot be valid.

The same goes for syllogisms in mood OO, since O statements are also negative. In fact, if we constructed syllogisms in all 64 of the possible combinations, and applied the seven rules we learned in Book I, we would find that only 19 of them are valid.

William of Shyreswood, a medieval philosopher, came up with names to help remember these syllogisms and put them into a mnemonic verse. You will need to memorize these lines in order to know how to do some logical operations in later chapters. The lines are as follows:

BARBARA, CELARENT, DARII, FERIOque prioris;
CESARE, CAMESTRES, FESTINO, BAROCO secundae;
Tertia; **DARAPTI, DISAMIS, DATISI, FELAPTON, BOCARDO, FERISON** habet;
quarta insuper addit; **BRAMANTIP, CAMENES, DIMARIS, FESAPO, FRESISON.**

Note that FERIOque is Latin for "and FERIO," and that the *que* attached on the end is not really a part of the word.

Both the vowels and the consonants in these names represent important things about each syllogism. Let us content ourselves in this chapter to discuss what is indicated by the vowels.

We label a syllogism **BARBARA** if the first premise is an A statement (the first **A** in B<u>A</u>RBARA), and the second premise is an A statement (the second **A** in BARB<u>A</u>RA). The last vowel (**A**) stands for the conclusion (the last **A** in BARBAR<u>A</u>).

Remember that the first vowel always indicates the first (or major) premise; the second always indicates the second (or minor) premise; and the final vowel always indicates the conclusion.

What the above lines mean is that BARBARA, CELARENT, DARII and FERIO are the four valid moods in the First Figure (*prioris* means *of the first* in Latin). CESARE, CAMESTRES, FESTINO and BAROCO are the valid moods in the Second Figure (*secundae* means *of the second* in Latin); DARAPTI, DISAMIS, DATISI, FELAPTON, BOCARDO and FERISON are the valid moods of the Third Figure (*tertia* means *third* in Latin); and BRAMANTIP, CAMENES, DIMARIS, FESAPO and FRESISON are the valid moods in the Fourth Figure (*quarta* means *fourth* in Latin). This makes 19 in all.

Of these 19, however, only about five are commonly encountered in actual argument. We will be discussing all 19 of these arguments in later chapters, but for now, let's take a look at the five common valid syllogisms.

_____ **How to Use the Mnemonic.** The mnemonic (BARBARA, CELARENT, DARII, etc.) gives us a much quicker way to determine the validity of a syllogism than using the seven rules for validity. When we are presented with an argument, we simply put it in the form of a syllogism and see if it is one of the syllogisms in the mnemonic. If it is, then it is valid; if it is not, then it is invalid. There are three steps involved:

Step #1: Determine the figure
Step #2: Determine the mood
Step #3: Determine whether the mood is included in the mnemonic verse.

_____ **Five common syllogisms.** The following are the five most commonly encountered syllogisms:

BARBARA
CELARENT
CESARE
CAMESTRES
CAMENES

An example of BARBARA (which is *sub-prae* or First Figure) would be:

All flowers are plants.	(A)
All roses are flowers	(A)
Therefore, all roses are plants.	(A)

Of the 19 valid syllogisms, only five are commonly used in actual argument.

An example of CELARENT (First Figure) would be:

No flowers are trees.	(E)
All roses are flowers.	(A)
Therefore, no roses are trees.	(E)

An example of CESARE (a Second Figure or *prae-prae* syllogism) would be:

No trees are flowers.	(E)
All roses are flowers.	(A)
Therefore, no roses are trees.	(E)

An example of CAMESTRES (Second Figure) would be:

All roses are flowers.	(A)
No trees are flowers.	(E)
Therefore, no trees are roses.	(E)

An example of CAMENES (a Fourth Figure, or *prae-sub*, syllogism) would be:

All roses are flowers.	(A)
No flowers are trees.	(E)
Therefore, no trees are roses.	(E)

Note also that the final letter is important in determining the syllogism's validity, although it does not determine the mood.

——————— **Summary.** This chapter concerns the *mood* of syllogisms. The mood of a syllogism is defined as *the disposition of the premises according to quantity and quality*. There are sixteen moods per figure. Since there are four figures, that means there are 64 moods in all. Of these moods, only 19 are valid.

William of Shyreswood came up with names to help remember the valid syllogisms in a mnemonic verse. The verse is as follows:

BARBARA, CELARENT, DARII, FERIOque prioris;
CESARE, CAMESTRES, FESTINO, BAROCO secundae;
Tertia; DARAPTI, DISAMIS, DATISI, FELAPTON, BOCARDO, FERISON habet;
quarta insuper addit; BRAMANTIP, CAMENES, DIMARIS, FESAPO, FRESISON.

The vowels in each of these names indicate the mood of the syllogism by indicating whether each proposition in the syllogism is an A, I, E or O statement.

Of the 19 valid syllogisms, only five are commonly encountered in actual argument. The five common syllogisms are as follows:

BARBARA
CELARENT
CESARE
CAMESTRES
CAMENES

When we are presented an argument, we simply put it in the form of a syllogism and see if it is one of the syllogisms in the mnemonic.

_____ **Exercises for Day 1.** **Peruse entire chapter. Then read the introductory section at the very beginning of the chapter. Read this section carefully and try to understand it as best you can.**

1. What are we discussing in this chapter?

2. Fill in the following chart [Review]:

> **First Figure (*sub-prae*)**
>
> M is the _____ (subject or predicate) in the *major* premise
>
> M is the _____ (subject or predicate) in the *minor* premise

3. Give the definition of *figure*.

4. Give the definition of *mood*.

5. How many figures are there?

6. How many different moods are there?

7. If we say that a syllogism is in the mood AA what do we mean?

8. If we say that a syllogism is in the mood EA what do we mean?

9. Indicate the mood of the following syllogism:

> All mortals must die   Mood: __ __
> All men are mortal
> Therefore, all men must die

10. Indicate the mood of the following syllogism:

> No men are immortal   Mood: __ __
> All angels are immortal
> Therefore, no angels are men

11. Using the letters A, E, I and O to indicate the kind of statements used as premises, write out the 16 possible moods.

_____ **Exercises for Day 2.** **Read the section titled, "Figure and Mood." Read the entire section carefully.**

12. Fill in the following chart [Review]:

> **Second Figure (*prae-prae*)**
>
> M is the _____ (subject or predicate) in the *major* premise
>
> M is the _____ (subject or predicate) in the *minor* premise

13. Can syllogisms of the same mood be in different figures (Can there be, for example, an AA syllogism in the First **and** Second Figure)?

14. With sixteen different moods and four different figures, how many possible kinds of syllogisms are there?

15. Give the name of at least one whole mood that is invalid.

16. Of the 64 different kinds of syllogisms, how many are valid?

17. Write out the lines invented by William of Shyreswood to remember the valid syllogisms.

18. What are the valid moods in the First Figure? (Indicate them both by their letters and their names.)

> Example: Barbara, AA; Celarent, EA; etc.

19. What are the valid moods in the Second Figure? (Indicate them both by their letters and their names.)

20. What are the valid moods in the Third Figure? (Indicate them both by their letters and their names.)

21. What are the valid moods in the Fourth Figure? (Indicate them both by their letters and their names.)

22. What do the vowels in these names indicate?

_____ **Exercises for Day 3.** **Read the section titled, "Five common syllogisms." Read the entire section carefully.**

23. Write out the lines invented by William of Shyreswood to remember the valid syllogisms. [Review]

24. Fill in the following chart: [Review]

> **Third Figure (sub-sub)**
>
> M is the _____ (subject or predicate) in the **major** premise
>
> M is the _____ (subject or predicate) in the **minor** premise

25. Of the kinds of syllogisms that can be valid, how many are commonly used?

26. Describe the five most commonly used syllogisms (i.e. tell what mood and figure they are in.)

27. What are the names for these commonly used syllogisms invented by William of Shyreswood?

Read section titled, "How to Use the Mnemonic." Read it carefully.

28. Give the three steps outlined in the text for determining the validity of a syllogism using the mnemonic presented in the text.

Tell what figure and mood these syllogisms are in. If it is valid, give the name. Use the three-step method you wrote for your answer in question 28 to help determine the names.

29.   No pernicious thing is commendable
        Some indulgence is a pernicious thing
        Therefore, some indulgence is not commendable
                Figure: _____
                Mood: _____
                Name: _____

30.   No man hates life
        All men are mortal
        Therefore, some mortals do not hate life
                Figure: _____
                Mood: _____
                Name: _____

31.   All living things breathe
        All plants are living things
        Therefore, all plants breathe
                Figure: _____
                Mood: _____
                Name: _____

32.   All jealous persons are bitter
        No saints are bitter
        Therefore, no saints are jealous persons
                Figure: _____
                Mood: _____
                Name: _____

33.   All that encourages evil is pernicious
        Some indulgence encourages evil
        Therefore, some indulgence is pernicious
                Figure: _____
                Mood: _____
                Name: _____

34.   No bitter man has peace
        All saints have peace
        Therefore, no saint is a bitter man
                Figure: _____
                Mood: _____
                Name: _____

_____ **Exercises for Day 4.** **Read the section titled, "Summary." Read the entire section carefully.**

35. Write out the lines invented by William of Shyreswood to remember the valid syllogisms.

36. Fill in the following chart: [Review]

Fourth Figure—Indirect First (*prae-sub*)

M is the _____ (subject or predicate) in the **major** premise

M is the _____ (subject or predicate) in the **minor** premise

37. What is the Latin saying invented to help remember the four figures? [Review]

38. What does this saying mean? [Review]

Tell what figure and mood these syllogisms are in and give the syllogistic name.

39.   All centaurs are half-man, half-horse
      All centaurs are fabulous beings
      Therefore, some fabulous beings are half-man, half-horse
            Figure: _____
            Mood: _____
            Name: _____

40.   All animals have a body
      Some animals are intelligent beings
      Therefore, some intelligent beings have bodies
            Figure: _____
            Mood: _____
            Name: _____

41.   All fools are annoying
      Some chatterboxes are not annoying
      Therefore, some chatterboxes are not fools
            Figure: _____
            Mood: _____
            Name: _____

42.   All flowers are plants
      Some beautiful things are flowers
      Therefore, some beautiful things are plants
            Figure: _____
            Mood: _____
            Name: _____

43.   Some mammals are dogs
      All dogs are friendly
      Therefore, some friendly things are mammals
            Figure: _____
            Mood: _____
            Name: _____

44. Complete the following diagram by giving the form of each statement and showing whether each term is distributed or undistributed: [Review]

DISTRIBUTION

Letter designation	Form (e.g. "All S is P")	Subject-Term	Predicate-Term
A	_____	_____	_____
I	_____	_____	_____
E	_____	_____	_____
O	_____	_____	_____

45. Think up your own syllogisms of the following forms:

BARBARA:
- _____
- _____
- _____

CELARENT:
- _____
- _____
- _____

CESARE:
- _____
- _____
- _____

CAMESTRES:
- _____
- _____
- _____

CAMENES:
- _____
- _____
- _____

46. Tell whether the following are true or false:

T	F	Mood is the disposition of terms in a syllogism.
T	F	The mood of a syllogism of the form CELARENT is EA.
T	F	There are sixteen moods per figure.
T	F	There are sixteen valid moods.
T	F	BARBARA, CELARENT, DARII and FERIO are valid syllogisms of the First Figure.
T	F	Syllogisms in the mood OO are always invalid.

He was in logic a great critic;
profoundly skill'd in Analytic;
He could distinguish and divide
A hair 'twixt south and south-west side.

—Samuel Butler

Reducing Syllogisms to the First Figure

_____ **Introduction.** In past chapters, we have discussed the four figures of the syllogism. The figure of a syllogism, remember, is the disposition or location of the terms in the premises. Syllogisms can be divided into four figures, according to where the middle term appears in each premise.

Of the four different figures, the First Figure is the most straightforward and the one in which the validity is the easiest to recognize. For this reason, logicians have found ways to transform syllogisms in the other four figures into syllogisms of the First Figure.

The study of how to reduce other kinds of syllogisms to the First Figure is also helpful in understanding the mechanics of the traditional syllogism. Once you are able to reduce Second, Third and Fourth (Indirect First) Figure syllogisms to the First Figure, you will understand syllogisms much better.

_____ **Two Methods of Reduction.** There are two ways this can be done:

✓ Direct Reduction
✓ Indirect Reduction

We will study the first kind of reduction, **_Direct Reduction_**, in this chapter. But first, let's consider the different operations we will use to reduce syllogisms of the Second, Third and Fourth Figure to the First Figure.

_____ **The Nineteen Valid Moods.** You will remember that out of the 64 different kinds of syllogisms (we know there are 64 because there are 16 different moods and 4 different figures) there are only 19 that are

There are two ways to reduce a syllogism in one of the other figures to the First Figure: Direct Reduction and Indirect Reduction.

valid. Let us review them so that we can demonstrate how to reduce syllogisms.

As we have seen, each valid syllogism has been given a name as follows:

BARBARA, CELARENT, DARII, FERIOque prioris;
CESARE, CAMESTRES, FESTINO, BAROCO secundae;
Tertia; **DARAPTI, DISAMIS, DATISI, FELAPTON, BOCARDO, FERISON** habet;
quarta insuper addit; **BRAMANTIP, CAMENES, DIMARIS, FESAPO, FRESISON.**

Remember that the vowels in each of these words indicate the mood of the syllogism. For example, BARBARA indicates an AA syllogism with a conclusion that is also an A statement.

The first consonant indicates the mood in the First Figure to which each valid syllogism in the Second, Third and Fourth Figure can be reduced.

_____ What the Consonants Mean. We know what the vowels in the words above mean, since we studied them in the last chapter, but what do the consonants in these words mean? The first consonant indicates the mood in the First Figure to which each valid syllogism in the Second, Third and Fourth Figure can be reduced. In other words, it tells you which kind of syllogism in the First Figure you should end up with after it has been reduced.

For example, notice that CESARE, a Second Figure syllogism, has the same first letter as CELARENT, a valid mood of the First Figure—both begin with *C*. That means that when a CESARE syllogism is reduced, it becomes a CELARENT syllogism. If, after you have done the reduction on a CESARE, it is NOT a CELARENT, then you know you have done something wrong. All syllogisms in figures other than the First that begin with C will reduce to a CELARENT if the reduction is done properly.

FESTINO, on the other hand, or any other syllogism in figures other than the First, whose names begins with *F*, must reduce to FERIO. Likewise, any syllogism whose name begins with *B* reduces to BARBARA. And any syllogism beginning with *D* reduces to DARII.

That takes care of what each non-First Figure syllogism must look like after it has been reduced to the First Figure. But how do you do a reduction?

_____ The Four Operations for Reduction. A reduction of a non-First Figure syllogism to a First Figure syllogism can be done in one of four ways. But how do you know which way to use? Once again, we look to the name of the argument to tell us. Which method you should use to reduce a syllogism to the First Figure is dictated by other consonants in the name of the syllogism. The letters *S*, *P*, *M* and *C*, when they appear in the body (i.e. not as the initial consonant) of the syllogism name, indicate which type of reduction procedure to use.

These operations are indicated as follows:

S: *Simple conversion* of the proposition signified by the preceding vowel;
P: *Per accidens*, or *partial* conversion of the proposition signified by the preceding vowel;
M: *Mutatio*, or *transposition of the premises*; make the minor premise the major, and the major the minor;
C: *Reduction by contradiction*. This is the indirect method of reduction through (rather than to) BARBARA. It is signified by a noninitial **c** and is applied only to BAROCO and BOCARDO.

This sounds complicated, but let's explain it by giving some examples. Let's take the following syllogism:

No fish^P is a mammal^M
All whales^S are mammals^M
Therefore, No whale^S is a fish^P

First we look to see what figure the syllogism is in. We see that the middle term, **mammal** is in the predicate in both the major and minor premise—it is **prae-prae**, a Second Figure syllogism.

Second, we look to see what mood the syllogism is in. We see that it is EA. What is the name for an EA syllogism in the Second Figure? It is CESARE. The first letter in the word CESARE—**C**—tells us that we will be converting this syllogism to CELARENT, its First Figure equivalent.

Third, we look to see which of the letters above which indicate the appropriate operations (S, P, M or C) appear in the name CESARE. We notice that there is an S: CE<u>S</u>ARE. We then look back at our chart on the previous page to see what S indicates we should do. It says, '**Simple Conversion** of the proposition signified by the preceding vowel.' We know therefore that we must convert the proposition signified by the vowel preceding the **S** in CESARE. Since **E** is the vowel that precedes the S in CESARE, and since the E is the first vowel in CESARE, we know that we must do a conversion of the major premise, which is an E statement.

In order to do this, we must remember what conversion is. We discussed this in Chapter 9 of Book I in which we covered the three ways of converting propositions to other equivalent propositions. Let us review it for a moment.

_____ **Review of Conversion.** We said in the previous book that there are three ways to convert statements to their logical equivalents: Obversion, Conversion and Contraposition. In the present case, in which we are trying to find out how to reduce CESARE, the **S** indicates we are to perform a Simple Conversion. This just means Conversion, as opposed to Obversion or Contraposition, the other two methods. In Conversion we simply interchange (or switch) the subject and the predicate—we place the predicate where the subject is and the subject where the predicate is.

_____ **Reduction Involving Conversion.** So let's interchange the subject and the predicate of our CESARE syllogism:

We start with:

No fish^P is a mammal^M CE
All whales^S are mammals^M SA
Therefore, No whale^S is a fish^P RE

After we convert the major premise, we end up with:

No mammal^M is a fish^P CEL
All whales^S are mammals^M AR
Therefore, No whale^S is a fish^P ENT

The letters S, P, M and C, when they appear in the body of the syllogism name, indicate which type of reduction procedure to use.

We see that whereas before we had a Second Figure syllogism (**prae-prae**), we now have a First Figure syllogism (**sub-prae**). Furthermore, they are logically the same syllogism, since in conversion we are changing one statement to another logically equivalent statement.

Let's try another one:

All men^M are mortal^P DAR
All men^M are bipeds^S AP
Therefore, some bipeds^S are mortal^P TI

This syllogism is a Third Figure syllogism—**sub-sub**. Its mood is AA. Now we know, by looking at the lines we gave above, that an AA syllogism in the third figure is DARAPTI. We see that this name has in it the letter **P**, which is one of the four letters (S, P, M and C) that indicate which operation we must perform in order to make the syllogism a First Figure syllogism. In the case of P, the operation is partial conversion of the proposition signified by the preceding vowel.

_____ **Review of Partial Conversion.** What is Partial Conversion? Partial Conversion is a kind of Conversion (again, as opposed to Obversion and Contraposition) in which an A statement can be partially converted into an I statement. A Partial Conversion is accomplished by interchanging the subject and predicate (just as in ordinary Conversion) and changing the quantity (i.e. changing it from a universal to a particular statement). If, for example, I say **All dogs are animals**, I can partially convert it by interchanging **dogs** and **animals** and making it particular. If I do this, I get **Some animals are dogs**.

_____ **Reduction Using Partial Conversion.** The proposition indicated by the vowel preceding P in DARAPTI is the minor premise, which we know to be an A statement:

We start with:

All men^M are mortal^P DAR
All men^M are bipeds^S AP
Therefore, some bipeds^S are mortal^P TI

And by partially converting the minor premise, we get:

All men^M are mortal^P DAR
Some bipeds^S are men^M I
Therefore, some bipeds^S are mortal^P I

Again, we see that we have an equivalent syllogism, even though it is a different mood in a different figure. And note that it is a First Figure DARII.

In order to reduce some syllogisms to the First Figure, more than one step must be taken.

_____ **Reduction Involving Multiple Steps.** In order to reduce some syllogisms to the First Figure, more than one step must be taken. This is indicated if the consonants S, P, M or C appear more than once in the name of the syllogism you are trying to reduce. Let's take a look at this one:

Some crows^M are carnivorous^P	DIS
All crows^M are birds^S	AM
Therefore, Some birds^S are carnivorous^P	IS

This is the Third Figure syllogism DISAMIS. It reduces to DARII, since it begins with D. But there are three operations you have to go through to accomplish this. Look at the word **DISAMIS**. It has three consonants that correspond to operations in the list we looked at above: DISAMIS. Does this indicate that we have to do three different things to this syllogism in order to reduce it to the First Figure? Yes, it does. The first S indicates Simple Conversion of the major premise, which is an I statement, since the S follows the I. The M indicates that we need to make the major premise the minor and the minor premise the major. The second S indicates that we do a Simple Conversion on the conclusion.

In what order is this done? It is done in the order in which the consonants appear. In other words, you do a simple conversion on the major premise first, then transpose (i.e. switch) the major and minor premises, and then do a simple conversion on the conclusion—in that order. It is very important that you observe this order because, if you do not, you will not end up with the correct First Figure syllogism.

Step one, then, would be to convert the major premise, **Some crows are carnivorous**. In doing so, we get **Some carnivorous things are crows**. Step Two involves transposing the major and minor premises, yielding the following:

All crows^M are birds^S
Some carnivorous things^M are crows^P
Therefore, some birds^S are carnivorous^P

We have one step left, which is to do a simple conversion on the conclusion, going from **Some birds are carnivorous** to **Some carnivorous things are birds**. Once this is done, we see, once again, that we now have a First Figure (**sub-prae**) syllogism—a DARII:

All crows^M are birds^P	DA
Some carnivorous things^S are crows^M	RI
Therefore, some carnivorous things^S are birds^P	I

We have covered S, P and M, but have not covered C, which involves Indirect Reduction. Since it involves a very different procedure, we will leave its explanation to the next chapter.

It is very important that you observe the order of reduction indicated by the relevant consonants because, if you do not, you will not end up with the correct First Figure syllogism.

In this chapter,
we discussed
ways to reduce
syllogisms of the
Second, Third
and Fourth
Figures to First
Figure
syllogisms.

────────── **Summary.** In this chapter, we discussed ways to reduce syllogisms of the Second, Third and Fourth Figures to First Figure syllogisms. We said that there are two kinds of reduction. The first is called **_Direct_** Reduction and the second is called **_Indirect_** Reduction. In this chapter we discussed Direct Reduction.

In addition to the vowels in the syllogism's names, some of the consonants also have a purpose. The consonants, S, P, M and C, when they appear in the body of a syllogism name, indicate four different methods by which a syllogism may be reduced to the First Figure. The method indicated by each of these letters is as follows:

S: *Simple conversion* of the proposition signified by the preceding vowel;
P: *Per accidens*, or *partial*, conversion of the proposition signified by the preceding vowel;
M: *Mutatio*, or *transposition of the premises*; make the minor premise the major, and the major the minor;
C: *Reduction by contradiction*. This is the indirect method of reduction through (rather than to) BARBARA. It is signified by a noninitial **c** and is applied only to BAROCO and BOCARDO.

When one of these consonants appears in the body of a syllogism name, it indicates that the operation it stands for must be performed on the proposition indicated by the preceding vowel.

Some non-First Figure syllogisms must be reduced to the First Figure by the use of multiple steps. We must use more than one step in any syllogism in which the letters S, P, M and C appear more than once. When more than one of these consonants appears, the operations they indicate must be performed in the order in which the consonants appear.

_____ **Exercises for Day I.** Peruse entire chapter. Then read the introductory section at the very beginning of the chapter. Read this section carefully and try to understand it as best you can.

1. What are we discussing in this chapter?

2. Explain what *figure* means. [Review]

3. How many figures are there? [Review]

4. Why would logicians want to transform syllogisms in the other three figures to syllogisms in the First Figure?

Read section titled, "Two Methods of Reduction." Read it carefully.

5. What are the two methods of reduction?

6. Which of these two methods of reduction are we studying in this chapter?

Read: Section titled, "The Nineteen Valid Moods." Read it carefully.

7. Give the names for the nineteen valid syllogisms as given by William of Shyreswood. [Review]

8. Give the names of the valid moods in the First Figure. [Review]

9. Give the names of the valid moods in the Second Figure. [Review]

10. Give the names of the valid moods in the Third Figure. [Review]

11. Give the names of the valid moods in the Fourth Figure. [Review]

12. What do the vowels in these names indicate? [Review]

_____ **Exercises for Day 2.** Read the section titled, "What the Consonants Mean." Read the entire section carefully.

13. Write out the 19 valid syllogisms as they are presented in the text. [Review]

14. What does the first letter in each of these names indicate?

15. To which syllogism in the First Figure does FESTINO reduce?

16. To which syllogism in the First Figure does DARAPTI reduce?

17. To which syllogism in the First Figure does CAMENES reduce?

18. To which syllogism in the First Figure does FERISON reduce?

Read section titled, "The Four Operations for Reduction." Read it carefully.

19. Explain what the consonants S, P, M and C indicate when they are found after the initial letter in syllogism names.

_____ **Exercises for Day 3.** **Review section titled, "The Four Operations for Reduction."**

Reduce the following syllogisms to the First Figure by following the procedure indicated:

20.   No philosophers are saints
          Some men are saints
          Therefore, some men are not philosophers

What figure is this syllogism in? (1st, 2nd, 3rd or 4th)

What mood is it in? (Write the name of the syllogism)

Which consonant (or consonants) tells you how to reduce to the First Figure?

What does it indicate you should do?

Write the syllogism after it has been reduced to the First Figure.

What mood is this syllogism now in? (give the name)

21.   No saints are philosophers
          Some saints are wise
          Therefore, some wise people are not philosophers

What figure is this syllogism in? (1st, 2nd, 3rd or 4th)

What mood is it in? (write the name of the syllogism)

Which consonant (or consonants) tells you how to reduce to the First Figure?

What does it indicate you should do?

Write the syllogism after it has been reduced to the First Figure.

What mood is this syllogism now in? (give the name)

22.   Some saints are philosophers
          All philosophers are men
          Therefore, some men are saints

What figure is this syllogism in? (1st, 2nd, 3rd or 4th)

What mood is it in? (write the name of the syllogism)

Which consonant (or consonants) tells you how to reduce to the First Figure?

What does it indicate you should do?

Write the syllogism after it has been reduced to the First Figure.

What mood is this syllogism now in? (give the name)

23.   No angels are men
        All philosophers are men
        Therefore, no philosophers are angels

        What figure is this syllogism in? (1st, 2nd, 3rd or 4th)

        What mood is it in? (write the name of the syllogism)

        Which consonant (or consonants) tells you how to reduce to the First Figure?

        What does it indicate you should do?

        Write the syllogism after it has been reduced to the First Figure.

        What mood is this syllogism now in? (give the name)

24.   Some men are wise
        All men are philosophers
        Therefore, some philosophers are wise

        What figure is this syllogism in? (1st, 2nd, 3rd or 4th)

        What mood is it in? (write the name of the syllogism)

        Which consonant (or consonants) tells you how to reduce to the First Figure?

        What does it indicate you should do?
        Write the syllogism after it has been reduced to the First Figure.

        What mood is this syllogism now in? (give the name)

25.   All saints are holy
        All saints are wise
        Therefore, some wise men are holy

        What figure is this syllogism in? (1st, 2nd, 3rd or 4th)

        What mood is it in? (write the name of the syllogism)

        Which consonant (or consonants) tells you how to reduce to the First Figure?

        What does it indicate you should do?

        Write the syllogism after it has been reduced to the First Figure.

        What mood is this syllogism now in? (give the name)

26.   No angels are men
        Some men are philosophers
        Therefore, some philosophers are not angels

        What figure is this syllogism in? (1st, 2nd, 3rd or 4th)

        What mood is it in? (write the name of the syllogism)

        Which consonant (or consonants) tells you how to reduce to the First Figure?

        What does it indicate you should do?

        Write the syllogism after it has been reduced to the First Figure.

        What mood is this syllogism now in? (give the name)

_____ Exercises for Day 4.

Reduce the following syllogisms to the First Figure, indicating the name of the First Figure syllogism it has been converted into (use the format for Day 3 exercises if necessary):

27.   All men are mortals
        Some men are Romans
        Therefore, some Romans are mortals

28.   No angels are men
        All men are mortal
        Therefore, some mortals are not angels

29.   Some mortals are men
        All men are sinners
        Therefore, some sinners are mortal

30.   All Romans are men
        No god is a man
        Therefore, no god is a Roman

31.   Some men are Romans
        All men are mortal
        Therefore, some mortals are Romans

32.   No men are gods
        All men are mortal
        Therefore, some mortals are not gods

33.   All Romans are men
        No men are gods
        Therefore, no gods are Romans

34. Tell whether the following are true or false:

T	F	There are four operations by which syllogisms can be reduced to the First Figure.
T	F	The consonants S, P, M and C, when found in the body of the name of a syllogism, indicate which figure the syllogism is in.
T	F	The consonant S indicates Simple Conversion of the proposition signified by the preceding vowel.
T	F	M indicates one of the methods of Direct Reduction.
T	F	C indicates one of the methods of Indirect Reduction.
T	F	M indicates that the reduction of the syllogism must be done in multiple steps.
T	F	Syllogisms in the Fourth (or Indirect First) Figure cannot be reduced to the First Figure.

"I believe in order to understand."
—St. Augustine

Indirect Reduction of Syllogisms

_____ **Introduction.** In the last chapter, we were able to take most of the moods from the Second, Third and Fourth Figures and reduce them to First Figure syllogisms. But there are two moods with which we cannot use Direct Reduction: these two moods are BAROCO and BOCARDO. With these moods, another method must be used: Indirect Reduction.

Remember that the reason we are reducing syllogisms to the First Figure in the first place is to see more easily that they are valid, since validity is more obvious in the First Figure. Since with BAROCO and BOCARDO we cannot do this, we must find another way to demonstrate their validity. This is the purpose of Indirect Reduction.

Let us first review the four operations we use in reduction:

S: *Simple Conversion* of the proposition signified by the preceding vowel;
P: *Per accidens*, or *Partial*, Conversion of the proposition signified by the preceding vowel;
M: *Mutatio,* or *Transposition of the Premises*; make the minor premise the major, and the major the minor;
C: *Reduction by Contradiction*. This is the indirect method of reduction through (rather than to) BARBARA. It is signified by a noninitial **c**, and is applied only to BAROCO and BOCARDO.

In Direct Reduction, we made use of the first three of these: S, P and M. Indirect Reduction, on the other hand, requires the use of C. In Direct Reduction, we transformed a Second, Third or Fourth Figure syllogism into a First Figure syllogism by changing the position of the middle term. But with syllogisms BAROCO and BOCARDO, this cannot be done.

Reduction by Contradiction is called *indirect* because it does not actually reduce the syllogism to a First Figure syllogism. What it does is prove that the syllogism is valid by *using* a First Figure syllogism. How is this done?

There are two moods with which we cannot use Direct Reduction: BAROCO and BOCARDO.

_____ **Indirect Reduction.** The ancient philosophers came up with a way to do this that was very clever. Let us first state the principle upon which this is based. It is as follows:

> *In a valid syllogism, if the conclusion is false, then at least one of the premises must be false.*

In order to show a syllogism to be valid, we make the conclusion false. If it forces us into denying one of the premises, we know then that it must be valid. In this way, we show that the syllogism is valid by showing that it cannot be invalid. We prove its validity by showing that its invalidity is impossible.

_____ **Indirect Reduction of BAROCO.** Let's try to do this on a syllogism in BAROCO to see how it works:

All rational creatures are created in the image of God	BAR
Some animals are not created in the image of God	OC
Therefore, some animals are not rational creatures	O

If this syllogism is valid, then when we deny the conclusion we should end up with a denial of one of the premises. If we say that all animals are rational creatures (thereby contradicting the conclusion), we should be able to derive the contradiction of at least one of the premises: either ***Some rational creatures are NOT created in the image of God*** (the contradiction of the major premise) or ***all animals are created in the image of God*** (the contradiction of the minor premise).

Under operation C in BAROCO above, we are told to use contradiction on the statement indicated by the vowel that precedes the ***C***. In BAROCO, that means the ***minor*** premise, which is an O statement. But, we don't replace the O statement with its own contradictory, we replace it with the contradictory of the conclusion. We do this by taking the contradiction of the conclusion and putting it in the place of our original minor premise. By doing this, we should get (if the argument is indeed valid), a contradiction of the original minor premise in the conclusion. Let us see if this happens.

Now in order to do this we must remember another principle we learned in a previous chapter. Remember the Rule of Contradiction? It said that ***contradictory statements are statements that differ both in quality and quantity*** (Remember that is different from contraries, in which both statements are universals, but differ only in quality). To help us remember, we will resurrect the chart of the relationships between the statements:

<u>Quality</u>

	Affirmative	**Negative**
Universal	A	E
Particular	I	O

<u>Quantity</u> appears to the left of Universal/Particular rows.

As you can see from the chart, the A statement contradicts the O statement and the I statement contradicts the E statement. Using this principle in our Indirect Reduction of BAROCO, we must replace the O statement that is the minor premise with an A statement that is the contradictory of our original conclusion.

The O statement that was the minor premise in our example syllogism is as follows:

> Some animals are not created in the image of God

When we replace it with the contradiction of the conclusion, we get:

> All animals are rational creatures

This gives us the following syllogism:

All rational creatures are created in the image of God	BAR
All animals are rational creatures	BAR
Therefore, all animals are created in the image of God	A

Notice that the conclusion has changed. It went from **Some animals are rational creatures** to **All animals are created in the image of God**, because that is the only conclusion you can come to from the two premises. Notice also that it is now a BARBARA, a First Figure syllogism. But more importantly, remember, we said that, if the argument is valid, we should end up with a conclusion that contradicts the minor premise. Did this happen? Our new conclusion is:

> All animals are created in the image of God

Does this contradict our original minor premise (**Some animals are not created in the image of God**)? It does, since one is an A statement and the other an O. Therefore, the original BAROCO argument is valid.

The method for indirectly reducing BAROCO, then, is basically a three-step method:

Step #1: Retain the original **major** premise
Step #2: Use the contradiction of the original conclusion as the new **minor** premise
Step #3: Derive the new conclusion, which, if the original syllogism is valid, should be the contradiction of the original **minor** premise

In BAROCO, if we take the contradiction of our original conclusion and put it in the place of the minor premise, we should derive the contradiction of our original minor premise.

_____ **Indirect Reduction of BOCARDO.** We do essentially the same thing with BOCARDO, a Third Figure, or *sub-sub* syllogism, except that we replace the major premise, rather than the minor, with the contradiction of the conclusion. Let's use the following as an example:

Some animals are not rational	BOC
All animals are created by God	AR
Therefore, some things that are created by God are not rational	DO

> **W**e do essentially the same thing with **BOCARDO,** except that we replace the major premise, rather than the minor, with the contradiction of the conclusion.

We look at the name of this syllogism, BOCARDO, and it should tell us what to do. We see that the C in BO<u>C</u>ARDO indicates that we replace the major premise with the contradiction of the conclusion. If it is valid, we should get, as our new conclusion, the contradiction of the original major premise:

All things that are created by God are rational	BAR
All animals are created by God	BAR
Therefore, all animals are rational	RA

Does *All animals are rational* (the new conclusion) contradict *Some animals are not rational* (the original major premise)? Yes, it does. Therefore this argument is valid.

The method for indirectly reducing BOCARDO, then, also involves a three-step method:

Step #1: Retain the original *minor* premise
Step #2: Use the contradiction of the original conclusion as the new *major* premise
Step #3: Derive the new conclusion, which, if the original syllogism is valid, should be the contradiction of the original *major* premise

We used the same reasoning as with BAROCO, but did it through the major, instead of the minor, premise. Notice once again that we ended up with a First Figure argument. Unlike in Direct Reduction, it is not the First Figure equivalent of our original argument, we just used it, indirectly, to show that our original argument was valid.

_____ **Summary.** The reason we reduce syllogisms to the First Figure is to make their validity more apparent, since validity is more obvious in the First Figure. There are two moods on which Direct Reduction doesn't work: BAROCO and BOCARDO. We must therefore use Indirect Reduction. Indirect Reduction is accomplished by replacing the O premises in BAROCO and BOCARDO with the contradiction of the conclusion. We replace the original conclusion with the statement that logically follows from the two new premises and, if that conclusion contradicts one of the original premises (the minor in BAROCO and the major in BOCARDO), then the original syllogism is valid.

_____ **Exercises for Day I.** **Peruse entire chapter. Then read the introductory section at the very beginning of the chapter. Read this section carefully and try to understand it as best you can.**

1. Explain each of the four methods of reduction. [Review]

2. What is the reason for reducing syllogisms to the First Figure in the first place?

3. Which two moods cannot be reduced to the First Figure by using Direct Reduction?

4. Which of the four operations (S, P, M and C) do you use in Indirect Reduction?

Read: "Indirect Reduction." Read it carefully.

5. Why is Reduction by Contradiction considered indirect rather than direct?

6. What is the principle upon which Indirect Reduction is based?

7. Under this method, if a syllogism is valid, what should we expect?

_____ **Exercises for Day 2.** **Read: "Indirect Reduction of BAROCO." Read it carefully.**

8. In the example BAROCO given in the book, if we say that all animals are rational creatures (thereby contradicting the conclusion of the original syllogism), what should we be able to derive at the end of our process of Indirect Reduction?

9. In BAROCO, which premise do we replace with the contradiction of the conclusion?

10. When the operation indicated in question 10 is completed, what statement do we have as our new conclusion?

11. What does this show?

12. Fill out the following chart: _____

	Affirmative	Negative
Universal	_____	_____
_____		
Particular	_____	_____

13. Which two sets of statements contradict one another?

14. In the example BAROCO in the book, what should the new conclusion be (i.e. what kind of statement, A, E, I or O)? Why?

15. What reasoning do we use in this procedure?

16. Give the three steps for the Indirect Reduction of BAROCO.

17. Indirectly Reduce the following syllogisms:

All tabbies are cats   All Morgans are horses
Some animals are not cats   Some animals are not horses
Therefore, some animals are not tabbies Therefore, some animals are not Morgans

_____ **Exercises for Day 3.** **Read section titled, "Indirect Reduction of BOCARDO."**
Read it carefully.

18. In the example BOCARDO given in the book, if we say that all things created by God are rational (thereby contradicting the conclusion of the original syllogism), what should we be able to derive at the end of our process of Indirect Reduction?

19. In BOCARDO, which premise do we replace with the contradiction of the conclusion of the original syllogism?

20. If this is done, what is the statement that you should get as your new conclusion?

21. What does this show?

22. Generally speaking, is the reasoning we use in this procedure any different from what we used with BAROCO?

23. Give the three steps for the Indirect Reduction of BOCARDO.

24. Indirectly Reduce the following syllogisms:

Some cats are not tabbies   Some horses are not Morgans
All cats are animals   All horses are animals
Therefore, some animals are not tabbies Therefore, some animals are not Morgans

Create a syllogism in each of the 19 valid moods (you may use the same three terms in all the syllogisms if you wish.) In doing so, follow this five-step procedure:

Step #1: Construct your conclusion first. Make sure you include the quantifier, a clearly expressed subject and predicate, and copula.
Step #2: Given the vowels in the name of the argument place the quantifiers at the beginning of the first two lines where you intend to put your premises.
Step #3: Determine the figure of the syllogism you are trying to construct, and place a space (you can use an underline if you wish) where the middle term should appear in the two premises, according to what figure it is in.
Step #4: Identify the minor and major terms (from the conclusion you have already written) and place them in the proper location in the premises.
Step #5: Fill in the blanks you left for your middle term with a term that makes the best sense in light of your minor and middle terms.

Example: Let's say we want to create a BARBARA. We apply **step #1** and write our conclusion:

All daisies are plants

We apply **step #2** and place the quantifiers, both of which in this case are **all**, since the first two vowels in B_A_RB_A_RA are **A**'s:

All
All
Therefore, all daisies are plants

According to **step #3**, then, we conclude that BARBARA is a First Figure syllogism, which means that the middle term is the **subject** of the major premise and the **predicate** of the minor premise. Therefore, we place a space indicating where the middle term should go:

All _____ are
All   are _____
Therefore, all daisies are plants

Then, applying **step #4**, we identify the **minor** term (the subject of the conclusion: **daisies**) and the **major** term (the predicate of the conclusion: **plants**) and place them in the appropriate spot in the premises:

All _____ are plants
All daisies are _____
Therefore, all daisies are plants

Finally, we apply **step #5** by selecting an appropriate middle term and placing it in both of the blank spaces:

All flowers are plants
All daisies are flowers
Therefore, all daisies are plants

This gives us a BARBARA. Now, try it on the following:

25. BARBARA
26. CELARENT
27. DARII
28. FERIO
29. CESARE
30. CAMESTRES
31. FESTINO
32. BAROCO
33. DARAPTI
34. DISAMIS

35. DATISI
36. FELAPTON
37. BOCARDO
38. FERISON
39. BRAMANTIP
40. CAMENES
41. DIMARIS
42. FESAPO
43. FRESISON

_____ **Exercises for Day 4.**

Indirectly reduce the following syllogisms (identify the mood, replace the O premise with the contradiction of the conclusion, and come up with the new conclusion):

44. All Athenians live in Greece
     Some Greeks do not live in Greece
     Therefore, some Greeks are not Athenians

45. Some Dorians are not Spartans
     All Dorians are Greeks
     Therefore, some Greeks are not Spartans

46. All Macedonians are barbarians
     Some Athenians are not barbarians
     Therefore, some Athenians are not Macedonians

47. Some laws are not written
     All laws are to be obeyed
     Therefore, some things to be obeyed are not written

48. All Spartans are soldiers
     Some Greeks are not soldiers
     Therefore, some Greeks are not Spartans

49. Take the syllogism that you thought up for FESTINO and directly reduce it to the appropriate First Figure mood.

50. Take the syllogism you thought up for DATISI and directly reduce it to the appropriate First Figure mood.

51. Take the syllogism you thought up for BRAMANTIP and directly reduce it to the appropriate First Figure mood.

52. Take the syllogism you thought up for CESARE and directly reduce it to the appropriate First Figure mood.

53. Take the syllogism you thought up for BAROCO and indirectly reduce it.

54. Take the syllogism you thought up for BOCARDO and indirectly reduce it.

Read section titled, "Summary." Read it carefully.

55. Tell whether the following are true or false:

T	F	The two moods in which Direct Reduction does not work are BARBARA and BAROCO.
T	F	In those cases in which Direct Reduction cannot be used, we must use Indirect Reduction.
T	F	The reason we reduce figures to the First is in order to more easily show them valid.
T	F	We indirectly reduce a syllogism by replacing the O premise with the contradiction of the original conclusion.
T	F	In Indirect Reduction, if the contradiction of the major premise also contradicts the contradiction of the minor premise, then the syllogism contradicts itself.

"There can never be any surprises in logic."
—Ludwig Wittgenstein

Translating Ordinary Sentences into Logical Statements

————————— **Introduction.** Up until now, we have been studying arguments that we have thought up out of thin air. We have been analyzing the *form* of syllogisms. But we seldom find arguments in the real world that are in the form of syllogisms. We must learn how to analyze arguments as they appear in everyday speech and writing.

It is sort of like cooking. Let's say we wanted to learn how to prepare a meal. We could go out and buy a TV dinner and put it in the oven. That's one way to prepare food—but it isn't really cooking. Whoever put the TV dinners together before they were put in the package was the real cook. But if all we had ever done was to cook TV dinners and were suddenly faced with having to cook a real meal, we would probably make a pretty good mess of it.

In one way, what we have been doing is preparing TV dinners—our arguments have mostly been prepared for you by someone else. Now this is not a perfect analogy, because we have been learning very important thinking skills by using these prepared arguments. But we do need to find out how arguments operate in the real world so we can use the skills we have learned productively.

In this chapter, we will learn how to translate ordinary statements into logical propositions so we can analyze them using the principles we have learned.

————————— **What a Statement Needs in Order to be a Logical Statement.** Ordinary sentences can have their logical components all scrambled up. In many cases, some of the components you need in a logical statement are simply missing, and you need to provide them. In other cases they are lost amidst a jumble of other words.

A logical proposition needs several things. It needs a *subject* and a *predicate*. It also needs a *quantifier*. A quantifier, remember, is a word such as *all*, *no*, or *some*. It needs a complete predicate, which sometimes involves adding a *complement*. It needs a *copula*, which links together the subject and the predicate. In logical sentences, this is the *to be* verb: *is*, *am*, or *are*.

> **I**n this chapter, we will learn how to translate ordinary statements into logical propositions so we can analyze them using the principles we have learned.

There are nine rules for translating ordinary sentences into logical statements.

_____ **Rules for Translating Sentences.** There are nine rules for translating ordinary sentences into logical statements:

> **Rule A:** Clearly identify the subject and predicate of the English sentence
> **Rule B:** Supply the missing quantifier
> **Rule C:** Add the missing complement
> **Rule D:** Supply the missing copula
> **Rule E:** Change exclusive sentences into A statements
> **Rule F:** Change negative sentences into E or O statements
> **Rule G:** Change exceptive sentences to E or A statements
> **Rule H:** Sentences containing **anyone**, **anything**, **whoever**, **the**, **if ... then**, **whatever** should be translated into A statements
> **Rule I:** Sentences containing **someone**, **something**, **there is**, or **there are** should be translated into I statements

_____ **Rule A: Clearly Identify the Subject and the Predicate.** This rule is somewhat self-explanatory. We identify the **subject**—the word that expresses what the sentence is about—and the **predicate**—the word that tells us something about the subject. Now let's look at a few examples:

> Seldom do taxpayers get a break
> A person takes a chance when he speaks out in public
> No one becomes a politician and keeps his integrity

In a logical sentence, the subject comes first. This is also the case many times in ordinary speech. But that is not the case in the sentences above. **Seldom**, in the first sentence, is not what the sentence is about; **taxpayers** is what the sentence is about. **Taxpayers** is therefore the subject. **People who seldom get a break** would, furthermore, be the predicate.

When the subject is put in its proper place (the beginning) and the predicate in its proper place (the end), we get:

> Taxpayers seldom get a break
> People who speak out in public take a chance
> No one who wants to keep his integrity becomes a politician

_____ **Rule B: Supply the Missing Quantifier.** A **quantifier** is the word that tells us the **quantity** of the statement. Words like **all**, **some** and **no** are quantifiers.

The general rule is that, unless the statement says specifically that **some** is meant, **all** is meant. In the three sentences we derived by applying Rule A, for example, we see that there are no quantifiers. We can easily provide them:

> All taxpayers seldom get a break
> All people who speak out in public take a chance
> No person who wants to keep his integrity becomes a politician

Some statements are a little less obvious. The statement:

> Socrates is a mortal

for example, is an A statement, even though it doesn't have the quantifier *all* in it. In logical terms, it really means:

> All persons indicated by the name **Socrates** are mortal

In this case that's only one person.

There are also some exceptions to the general rule. Take this one:

> Americans are great basketball players

Even though it does not say **some** explicitly, it is clear that we are not talking about all Americans. Therefore, it must be written in logical terms like this:

> Some Americans are great basketball players

Let's also look at an example having to do with the negative quantifier **no**:

> There aren't any boys in the room

This one should be rendered:

> No boys are in the room

_____ **Rule C: Add the Missing Complement.** Many times we encounter sentences in which the predicate is an adjective:

> All taxpayers are poor
> All people who speak out in public are brave
> No person who wants to keep his integrity is political

But we must remember that, in logic, we refer to classes of things. When we say, **All men are mortal**, we are referring to all members of the class we call **men** and to some subset of the class we call **mortal**. And when we say, **Socrates is a man**, we refer to the class we call **Socrates** (a class with only one member), and some subset of the class **men**.

When translating ordinary statements into logical sentences, we must remember to refer to them as classes. We do this by adding a **complement**, which is **a word or group of words that completes the predicate**.

Therefore, when we encounter an adjective, we must change it a little to make sure we specify the class about which we are talking. The sentences above, for example, become:

> All taxpayers are **poor people**
> All public speakers are **brave people**
> No person who wants to keep his integrity is a political **person**

When translating ordinary language statements into logical sentences, we must remember to refer to them as classes.

In these examples, the word ***persons*** is the complement. Likewise, the sentence:

All daffodils are yellow

should be rendered:

All daffodils are yellow ***flowers*** or ***plants*** or ***things***

In this last example, the class referred to is not completely clear. It could be flowers or plants or things. In the three previous examples, on the other hand, it is clear that the class (who are poor, brave or political) is people (or persons). In this chapter we will be very explicit about identifying the class even when it is not necessary, as in the first three examples.

_____ **Rule D: Supply the Missing Copula.** A ***copula*** is a word that links together the ***subject*** and the ***predicate***. In logical sentences, the copula means the ***to be*** verb; in other words ***is***, ***am*** or ***are***.

Notice that when we applied Rule C, we also added a copula:

All taxpayers ***are*** poor people
All public speakers ***are*** brave people
No person who wants to keep his integrity ***is*** a political person

When, for example, we take the sentence:

Dogs bark

we notice it is missing the copula. But if we add the missing copula (and the missing quantifier and missing complement—see Rule C), we get:

All dogs ***are barking animals***

Be aware that both Rules C and D are not often strictly followed even in the examples given in this book. It will be extremely useful to know them, even if you do not strictly follow them in every instance.

_____ **Rule E: Change Exclusive Sentences into A statements.**
Sometimes you run across a sentence that begins with the word ***only***. Like this one:

Only men are priests

What do we do with a sentence like this? It cannot mean ***All men are priests***. So what does it mean? In logical terms what it means is ***All priests are men***.

Whenever we encounter a sentence like this, we must do two things:

✓ Drop the word ***only*** (or ***none but***) and replace it by ***all***;

✓ Interchange the subject and predicate terms.

In the above sentence, therefore, we would take the sentence:

Only men are priests

and drop *only* and replace it by *all*, giving us:

All men are priests

We would then interchange the subject (*men*) and the predicate (*priests*), giving us:

All priests are men

_____ **Rule F: Change Negative Sentences into E or O Statements.** We translate ordinary sentences beginning with the words *nothing*, *none*, or *no one* by doing three things:

   ✓ Replace the words *nothing*, *none*, or *no one* with the word, *no* before the subject of the sentence;

   ✓ Add the copula;

   ✓ Complement the predicate.

Let's try it on a sentence. Let's take:

No one frightens me

We replace *no one* with *no*, we add the copula *is* and also add the missing complement. Then we get:

No persons are persons who frighten me

We should also point out that English sentences of the form *All . . . are not* are ambiguous; in other words, it is hard to tell how we should say them logically. Some of them should be E statements, and others should be O statements. For example, the sentence:

All people are not honest

could mean either *No people are honest* or *Some people are not honest*, but most likely it means *Some people are not honest*. The general rule is that we should always interpret such a sentence as an O statement unless it is clearly intended as an E statement.

_____ **Rule G: Change Exceptive Sentences to E or A statements.** There are some sentences that contain the word, *except*. Unfortunately, these sentences cannot be directly translated into A, E, I or O statements.

For example:

> Everyone except children may attend

By this we mean, not one, but two things:

> No children are people who are able to attend; *and*

> All who are not children are people who may attend

One of these is, of course, an E statement and the other an A statement.

But if this one statement was intended to be a premise in an argument, we are faced with a difficulty, since, in a categorical syllogism, there can only be two premises. But if one of our propositions was actually two, we would end up with three premises.

Therefore, the rule is that ***only one of the resulting statements may be used, but not both***. Any valid argument that contains an exceptive sentence will remain valid regardless of which is used.

_____ **Rule H: Sentences Containing *anyone, anything, whoever, the, if, if...then* or *whatever* Should be Translated into A Statements.**

> Anyone who has eyes can see
> Anything that has eyes can see
> Whoever has eyes can see
> The person who has eyes can see
> If a person has eyes, then he can see
> Whatever has eyes can see

Any one of these statements can be translated into the statement:

> All persons with eyes are persons who can see

_____ **Rule I: Sentences Containing *someone, something, there is,* or *there are* Should be Translated into I Statements.** All statements containing these words can be translated into I statements.

These statements:

> Someone is looking at me
> Something is looking at me
> There is a thing looking at me
> There are things looking at me

can all be translated into the statement:

> Some persons are persons who are looking at me; or

> Some things are things that are looking at me

Although these rules will not cover every kind of statement, they should enable you to translate most statements you come across into logical propositions. Remember also, that some sentences cannot be translated into logical statements (questions, commands, exhortations, etc.), since they do not express a judgement; they express other things. Only sentences that express judgements can be statements.

_____ **Summary.** In this chapter, we cover nine rules for translating ordinary language sentences into logical statements. Generally speaking, a logical proposition needs several things. It needs a **subject** and a **predicate**. It needs a **quantifier**, a complete **predicate**, which sometimes involves adding a **complement**. It needs a **copula** (a form of the **to be** verb), which links together the **subject** and the **predicate**.

Some sentences, however, cannot be translated into logical statements because they do not express judgements (questions, commands, exhortations, etc.).

_____ **Exercises for Day 1.** **Peruse the entire chapter. Then read the introductory** section at the very beginning of the chapter. Read this section carefully and try to understand it as best you can.

1. What do we learn in this chapter?

2. Why do ordinary sentences need to be translated in order to become logical statements?

Read "What a Statement Needs in Order to be Logical." Read it carefully.

3. List the components which a logical proposition should have.

Read sections concerning Rules A-D. Read them carefully.

4. Rewrite the following sentences using Rules A, B, C and D. Indicate which rules you used with each one.

> Abortion should be illegal
> A society that loses its moral bearings seldom survives
> Giving trade privileges to countries that violate human rights is wrong
> Television viewing is harmful to your health

5. Think of three sentences similar to the ones used in the discussion of Rule A, B, C and D (try to think of simple sentences with as few words as possible) and apply these three rules (circle the subject and write *S*; circle the predicate and write *P* in each one of your sentences) and then write out the statement in its proper logical form.

_____ **Exercises for Day 2.** **Read section titled, "Rule E: Change Exclusive Sentences** into A Statements." Read it carefully.

6. Explain Rule E in your own words.

Read: "Rule F: Change Negative Sentences into E or O Statements." Read it carefully.

7. Explain Rule F in your own words.

8. Rewrite the following sentences using Rules A, B, C, D, E and F.

> Guns do not cause crime
> Only people who haven't read the Consititution believe that it prohibits prayer in schools
> No one really believes animals have the same rights as humans
> No country that pollutes its environment can survive
> Without foreign aid from the United States many countries could not feed their own people

9. Think of three commonly used sentences (try to think of simple sentences with as few words as possible) and apply these five rules you have learned (circle the subject and write *S*; circle the predicate and write *P* in each one of your sentences) and then write out the statement in its proper logical form.

_____ **Exercises for Day 3.** Read: "Rule G: Change Exceptive Sentences into E or A Statements." **Read it carefully.**

10. Explain Rule G in your own words.

Read: "Rule H: Sentences Containing *anyone, anything, whoever, the, if ... then* or *whatever* **Should be Translated into A statements." Read it carefully.**

11. Explain Rule H in your own words.

12. Think of three sentences similar to the ones used in this section of the book and apply Rule H.

Read: "Rule I: Sentences Containing *someone, something, there is,* or *there are* **Should be Translated into I statements." Read it carefully.**

13. Explain Rule I in your own words.

14. Think of three sentences similar to the ones used in this section of the book and apply Rule I.

15. Rewrite the following sentences using all the rules you have learned:

> Anyone who thinks welfare helps people doesn't know what he's talking about
> There is no good evidence that poverty causes crime
> If public schools were doing a good job, there wouldn't be so many people homeschooling
> Whoever said that America is a melting pot never anticipated today's level of illegal immigration
> Someone should do something about the size of the government.

16. Think of three more commonly used sentences (try to think of simple sentences with as few words as possible) and apply these nine rules you have learned.

_____ **Exercises for Day 4.**

17. Rewrite the following sentences using all the rules you have learned:

> "Man shall not live by bread alone." (Matt. 4:4)
> "To everything there is a season." (Eccl. 3:1)
> "No man can serve two masters." (Matt. 6:24)
> "A foolish son is the heaviness of his mother." (Prov. 10:1)
> "No man hath ascended up to heaven, but he that came down from heaven." (John 3:13)
> "Liars shall have their part in the lake which burns with fire and brimstone." (Rev. 19:20)
> "Without Him was not anything made that was made." (John 1:3)

18. Rewrite the following sentences using all the rules you have learned. Note that all of them are examples of Rule E, rather than Rule G, as one might first think. You will also need to apply contraposition from Chapter 9 of Book I to solve them:

> "Except a man be born again, he cannot see the Kingdom of God."
> **—John 3:3**

"For I say unto you, that except your righteousness shall exceed the righteousness of the scribes and the Pharisees, ye shall in no case enter into the Kingdom of heaven."
   —Matthew 5:23

"Verily, verily I say unto you, except you eat the flesh of the Son of Man, and drink his blood, ye have no life in you."
   —John 6:30

19. Formulate syllogisms in the following moods using terms from any one or more of the statements in Exercise 4, 8, and 15 above and reduce them to the First Figure. Be sure they comply with the rules you learned in this chapter [Review]:

DISAMIS
DATISI
FELAPTON
BOCARDO
FERISON
BRAMANTIP
CAMENES
DIMARIS
FESAPO
FRESISON

Read section titled, "Summary." Read it carefully.

20. Tell whether the following are true or false:

T	F	A quantifier is a form of the to be verb .
T	F	The complement is a word that links together a subject and a predicate.
T	F	Exclusive sentences should be changed into A statements.
T	F	An exceptive statement needs only a complement.
T	F	The word *all* is a quantifier.

_____ **Weekly Analysis Assignment. Find an article from a newspaper (letters to the editor in newspapers are ideal) or magazine or a chapter from a book you are reading that contains any of the argument forms discussed in previous chapters. Either write a short 1-2 page essay or make a presentation in class analyzing the argument or arguments you have found. The paper or presentation should contain the following elements:**

1. A *presentation* of the argument as it was originally written.
2. A *summary* of the argument in your own words.
3. An *analysis* of the logical form of the argument.
4. An *evaluation* of the argument's soundness. This will involve assessing both the truth of the argument's premises and its validity. Remember that if the argument is valid and the premises are true, the conclusion must be true. If the argument is valid and one or more of the premises are false, then the conclusion must also be false. And if the argument is invalid, the truth of the conclusion cannot be determined one way or another by knowing the truth of the premises.
5. State your agreement or disagreement with the argument you have analyzed.

"Logic: The art of thinking and reasoning in strict accordance with the limitations and incapacities of the human misunderstanding."

—Ambrose Bierce

Enthymemes

_____ **Introduction.** When we encounter arguments in the normal course of conversation, we very rarely encounter them in the form of syllogisms as we have been studying them. Instead, we find arguments stated in a different form, requiring us to translate them into syllogisms ourselves—or to ask our opponent to do it in order to further explain himself.

In the last chapter, we discussed various ways to convert statements as we might hear them in normal conversation into logical propositions. In this chapter, we will discuss the most common way in which arguments are stated in ordinary conversation and how to convert such arguments into regular syllogisms. Doing this will allow us better to assess the arguments of our opponents.

_____ **What is an Enthymeme?** The most common way to express an argument is in the form of an *enthymeme* (pronounced, *en' thuh meem*). An enthymeme is a syllogism that does not contain both of the necessary premises—or contains both of its premises but is missing a conclusion. The missing premise or conclusion is implied, but not stated.

For example, let's take the following syllogism:

Atheists are people who disbelieve in God
John is an atheist
Therefore, John disbelieves in God

If we were to use this argument in ordinary conversation, we would probably say it this way:

John is an atheist
Therefore, John disbelieves in God

We would say it this way because we would naturally assume that whoever we were talking to would know what an atheist is: namely, a person who does not believe in God. Therefore, we would not bother to use the first (or major) premise.

An enthymeme is a syllogism that does not contain both of the necessary premises—or contains both of its premises but is missing a conclusion.

This is the most common reason for using enthymemes: that it is unnecessary to use one of the premises because we assume that one of the premises is common knowledge, eliminating the need to state it.

_____ **Three Kinds of Enthymemes.** There are three kinds of enthymemes, as follows:

- ✓ **First Order** enthymemes
- ✓ **Second Order** enthymemes
- ✓ **Third Order** enthymemes

Enthymemes are distinguished by which proposition they are missing.

These different kinds of enthymemes are distinguished on the basis of which proposition they are missing.

_____ **First Order Enthymemes.** Enthymemes of the **First Order** are distinguished by the fact that they are missing the **major premise**. The syllogism on the previous page is an example of a First Order enthymeme. In this argument:

All atheists^M are people who disbelieve in God^P
John^S is an atheist^M
Therefore, John^S disbelieves in God^P

we see that **All atheists are people who disbelieve in God** is the major premise (because it contains the major term). Therefore, the enthymeme:

John is an atheist
Therefore, John disbelieves in God

is an enthymeme of the First Order. It eliminates the major premise because it assumes that the hearer already knows it.

_____ **Second Order Enthymemes.** Enthymemes of the **Second Order** are distinguished by the fact that they are missing the **minor premise**. An example of this would be the following enthymeme:

Greek generals are people who are skilled in battle
Therefore, Alexander (the Great) is skilled in battle

What is missing here? What is missing is the premise, **Alexander the Great is a Greek general**. This is the minor premise (because it contains the minor term). We didn't include it because we assumed that the person we were talking to would know that Alexander was a Greek general. The complete syllogism would look like this:

Greek generals^M are people who are skilled in battle.^{P}
Alexander the Great^S is a Greek general.^{M}
Therefore, Alexander the Great^S is a person who is skilled in battle.^{P}

_____ **Third Order Enthymemes.** Enthymemes of the ***Third Order*** are enthymemes in which the conclusion, rather than either of the two premises, is missing. There are two reasons for enthymemes of the Third Order. The first is the use of the rhetorical device called ***innuendo***. Innuendo is when you want your listener to see the force of a logical conclusion by stating the premises for him and letting him draw the obvious conclusion.

The second reason involves logical exercises by which you want a student to be able to practice his logical skills by drawing a logical conclusion from two premises.

An example of a Third Order enthymeme for the purpose of innuendo would be the following:

> Homework is due on Monday
> And today is Monday

The conclusion the hearer is obviously supposed to draw is ***Therefore, homework is due today***.

_____ **How to Use Enthymemes.** When encountering enthymemes of the First and Second Order in arguments with another person, there are two things you can do:

✓ Point out the missing premise yourself; or
✓ Ask your opponent to state the missing premise

If your opponent uses an enthymeme to hide a faulty premise, you can state what the missing premise is, and point out that either the premise is false, or that the complete syllogism is invalid.

You can also ask your opponent to state the missing premise. This is useful when the argument is so clearly fallacious or the missing premise so clearly false that your opponent will be embarrassed to say it himself.

_____ **Summary.** An ***enthymeme*** is the most common form of an argument. An enthymeme is an argument that does not contain one of its premises, or which is missing the conclusion. There are three kinds or ***orders*** of enthymemes. In ***First Order*** enthymemes, the major premise is missing. In ***Second Order*** enthymemes, the minor premise is missing. In ***Third Order*** enthymemes, the conclusion is missing.

Premises (and conclusions) are sometimes dropped from arguments because it is assumed the hearers already know them and that it is therefore unecessary to state them.

In actual argument you can either point out the missing premise or conclusion yourself or ask your opponent to state it himself.

If your opponent uses an enthymeme to hide a faulty premise, you can point it out yourself or have him state the premise himself.

Enthymemes

Order:	Characteristic:
First	Missing **major** premise
Second	Missing **minor** premise
Third	Missing *conclusion*

How to Use Enthymemes:

✓ Point out the missing premise yourself

✓ Ask your opponent to state the missing premise

_____ **Exercises for Day 1.** **Peruse: Entire chapter. Then read the introductory section. Read it carefully.**

1. What is this chapter about?

2. Why is it important for us to know the material in this chapter?

3. In what form is an argument most commonly expressed?

Read section titled, "What is an Enthymeme?" Read it carefully.

4. What is the definition of an enthymeme?

5. Why would you not express one of the premises in an argument?

Read section titled, "Three Kinds of Ethymemes." Read it carefully.

6. What are the three kinds of enthymemes?

7. Upon what basis are these different kinds of enthymemes distinguished?

Read section titled, "First Order Enthymemes." Read it carefully.

8. Explain what a First Order enthymeme is in your own words.

Read section titled, "Second Order Enthymemes." Read it carefully.

9. Explain what a Second Order enthymeme is in your own words.

Read section titled, "Third Order Enthymemes." Read it carefully.

10. Explain what a Third Order Enthymeme is in your own words.

11. What two reasons are there for using a Third Order enthymeme?

_____ **Exercises for Day 2.**

12. Indicate the order of each of the following enthymemes:

> Abortion is the taking of an innocent life
> Therefore abortion is wrong

> Teen pregnancy hampers your ability to get an education
> And you have to have an education to be successful in life

> We shouldn't give special trade privileges to countries that violate human rights
> Therefore, we should not give China special trade privileges

> Activities that are psychologically damaging should be avoided
> And television is psychologically damaging

If something doesn't cause crime, then it shouldn't be banned
And guns don't cause crime

The Constitution does not prohibit school prayer
Therefore, it should not be outlawed

Animals are not the same as human beings
Therefore, animals should not have the same rights as humans

America is cleaning up its rivers and forests
Therefore, it will survive

A government takeover of the health care industry would cause a decline in the quality of care
Therefore, we should not let the government take over the health care industry

No welfare program that does not stress work can be effective
And our welfare programs stress work

All proof must be convincing
Therefore, there is no proof that poverty causes crime

If people are really concerned about their kids, they will avoid the public schools
And there are a lot of people avoiding the public schools

Any country that does not control its borders is destined for extinction
Therefore, America is destined for extinction

When the size of government spins out of control, personal liberties are endangered
Therefore, our personal liberties are endangered

13. Create three First Order enthymemes of your own.

——————— **Exercises for Day 3.**

14. Provide the missing premise and give the name of the syllogism (BARBARA, CELARENT, etc.) for each of the enthymemes in question 12. Or, if the syllogism is invalid, say which of the seven rules from Book I it violates (Note that on the 5th syllogism in 12. the negated terms require you to use contraposition to get the correct major premise and obversion to yield the correct minor premise; the 10th argument will require the use of obversion in the major premise).

15. Create three Second Order enthymemes of your own.

16. Do the following things with the given enthymemes:

    1) Put each of the two premises or conclusion into proper logical form;
    2) Supply the missing premise or conclusion;
    3) Tell what kind of enthymeme it is (i.e. First, Second or Third Order);
    4) Give the figure of the resulting complete syllogism;
    5) Give the name of the mood (e.g. BARBARA, etc.).

"I loathe my very life; therefore I will give free rein to my complaint and speak out in the bitterness of my soul."
> —Job 10:1

"Good and upright is the LORD: therefore will he teach sinners in the way."
> —Psalm 25:8

"Knowing this first, that no prophecy of the scripture is of any private interpretation. For the prophecy came not in old time by the will of man: but holy men of God spake as they were moved by the Holy Ghost.
> —I Peter 1:20,21

_____ **Exercises for Day 4.** **Read: Section titled, "Summary." Read it carefully.**

17. Take all the non-First Figure syllogisms you identified in question 12 and reduce them to the First Figure.

18. Create three Third Order enthymemes of your own.

19. Tell whether the following are true or false:

T	F	An enthymeme is the most common argument form .
T	F	All enthymemes are missing a conclusion.
T	F	A Third Order enthymeme is a syllogism that is missing a minor premise.
T	F	Enthymemes are missing one statement in the argument because the statement is logically unnecessary for the argument to be valid.

_____ **Weekly Analysis Assignment.** **Find an article from a newspaper (letters to the editor in newspapers are ideal) or magazine or a chapter from a book you are reading that contains enthymemes. This should be fairly easy, since most arguments are stated in this form. Either write a short 1-page essay or make a presentation in class analyzing the enthymeme. The paper or presentation should contain the following elements:**

1. A *presentation* of the enthymeme as it was originally written.
2. An *identification* of what kind of enthymeme it is.
3. A *summary* of the full argument implied by the enthymeme in your own words.
3. An *analysis* of the logical form of the full argument.
4. An *evaluation* of the full argument's soundness. This will involve assessing both the truth of the argument's premises and its validity. Remember that if the argument is valid and the premises are true, the conclusion must be true. If the argument is valid and one or more of the premises are false, then the conclusion must also be false. And if the argument is invalid, the truth of the conclusion cannot be determined one way or another by knowing the truth of the premises.
5. State your agreement or disagreement with the argument you have analyzed.

Rene Descartes

"I think, therefore I am"

_____The Argument in Plain Language: "I know I exist because I know I exist."

_____The Argument: "I think, therefore, I am."
—**Rene Descartes, *Discourse on Method*, Part IV**

_____**Background of the Argument:** One of the most discussed issues in the history of thought is that concerning the foundation of knowledge. How do we know anything? To this question, Rene Descartes, a 17th century philosopher, answered, I know at least this: that I think. And if I think, then I must exist. Descartes is considered to mark the transition from the Middle Ages to the "modern" world. Yet Descartes' ideas were founded on ideas much older than himself. In fact, the argument we study here, sometimes known simply as "the cogito" (from its Latin formulation: *cogito ergo sum*), was thought of long before he ever entered the world. Aristotle, who wrote almost 2,000 years before the birth of Descartes, is quoted by St. Thomas Aquinas (a 13th century philosopher) saying, "We sense that we sense, and we understand that we understand; and because we sense this, we understand that we exist." Descartes' formulation is admittedly a little snappier. All the same, it goes to prove once again that there is nothing new under the sun.

_____**Assignment:**
1. Formulate the argument in one simple syllogism, supplying the missing premise.
2. Write a 1-2 page essay explaining why you think the argument is sound or unsound. Give reasons for your conclusion. You might look up the word "epistemology" in a good encyclopedia (try www.Brittanica.com). *Epistemology* is the study of how we know what we know.
3. Write a short biographical essay on Rene Descartes.

_____**A little light humor at Descartes' expense:** If "cogito ergo sum" means "I think, therefore, I am," then does "cogito ergo sub" mean, "I think I'll have a sandwich"? Or how about, "cogito eggo sum": "I think, therefore I am a waffle"? Could "cogito ergo summit" be, "I think I'm at the top of a mountain"? Then there is our personal favorite, "cogito ergo sumo": "I'm wrestling with my thoughts."

"Somebody who thinks logically is a nice contrast to the real world."
—The Law of Thumb

Hypothetical Syllogisms

Conditional Syllogisms

_____ **Introduction.** In previous chapters of this book and in Book I, we have discussed the categorical syllogism. The validity of categorical syllogisms depends upon the relationships among the terms in the syllogism. The rules governing the validity of categorical syllogisms were covered in Chapters 11-13 of Book I.

Now, however, we begin the study of the *hypothetical* syllogism, which has rules and modes that are completely different from those of categorical syllogisms. The validity of hypothetical syllogisms depends upon the relationship, not among the *terms* in the syllogism, but among the *propositions* in the syllogism.

In categorical reasoning, we connect two concepts together (represented by the minor and major terms) by means of a third concept (represented by the middle term). In doing so we go from the two propositions set forth in the two premises to a new proposition set forth in the conclusion.

In hypothetical reasoning, we affirm or deny a judgement in the conclusion by affirming or denying one of the judgements set forth in the premises. A hypothetical syllogism is a syllogism the first premise of which is a complex, sequential proposition, one member of which is affirmed or denied in the second premise, and the other member of which is consequently affirmed or denied in the conclusion.

The rules for hypothetical syllogisms are completely different from those of categorical syllogisms.

_____ **Types of Hypothetical Syllogisms.** There are three kinds of hypothetical syllogisms. We will discuss only the first of these in this chapter. We will discuss the others in subsequent chapters. The three kinds of hypothetical syllogisms are as follows:

> **T**he validity of hypothetical syllogisms depends upon the relationship, not among the terms in the syllogism, but among the propositions.

✓ The conditional
✓ The disjunctive
✓ The conjunctive

_____ **Conditional Syllogisms.** A conditional syllogism is a syllogism that contains a conditional statement as its major premise, a categorical statement affirming or denying one of the elements of the conditional statement as its minor premise and a categorical statement affirming or denying one of the elements of the major premise as a conclusion.

An example of a conditional syllogism is as follows:

> If Christ rose from the dead, then Christ is God
> Christ rose from the dead
> Therefore, Christ is God

In this syllogism, the first premise is a hypothetical proposition; it is of the form **if ... then**. The second premise is a categorical proposition like the ones we have encountered studying categorical syllogisms in previous chapters. We don't see the copula in the proposition in the second premise as we should, that is true; but we can easily reformulate it using the rules for translating ordinary language statements into logical statements (in which case, we would get **Christ is a person who rose from the dead**).

A Note on Notation: When we were discussing the categorical syllogism, we sometimes reduced the terms to letters in order to make the form of the argument clearer. We sometimes wrote something like:

> M is P
> S is M
> Therefore, S is P

The letters here represent terms. But, in order to remind us of the difference between categorical and hypothetical syllogism, we will use a different notation for hypotheticals. We said that in hypothetical reasoning the logical units are no longer **terms**, but **propositions**. In analysing the form of hypothetical reasoning, we will use different letters to represent the propositions than we did for terms in categorical reasoning. Instead of using **S**, **P**, and **M**, we will use the letters **P**, and **Q**.

In regard to the hypothetical syllogism above, for the proposition

> Christ rose from the dead

we will use the letter **P**. For the proposition

> Christ is God

we will use the letter **Q**.

So when we use a conditional statement like,

> If Christ rose from the dead, then Christ is God

A conditional syllogism is a syllogism that contains a conditional statement as its major premise, a categorical statement affirming or denying one of the elements of the conditional statement as its minor premise, and a categorical statement affirming or denying one of the elements of the major premise as a conclusion.

we can reduce it, using the new letters, to:

If P, then Q

Let's go back to our example conditional syllogism on the previous page. Putting this into the new notation, we get:

If P, then Q
P
Therefore, Q

_____ **Terms and Premises in Hypothetical Syllogisms.** Notice that the terms represented by P and Q are not *terms* in the same sense as those in categorical syllogisms. There is no major term, minor term and middle term. This is because, again, hypothetical reasoning deals in propositions, not terms. Consequently, when we refer to *terms* in the context of hypothetical syllogisms, we are really referring to whole propositions which we represent by the letters P, Q, etc.

In addition, we will also make reference to the *major* and *minor* premises of a hypothetical syllogism. When we say this, we are using those phrases differently from the way we have been using them in discussing categorical syllogisms. In categorical syllogisms, the major premise is the premise which contains the major term, and the minor premise is the premise that contains the minor term. But in hypothetical syllogisms, there are no major and minor terms.

In hypothetical syllogisms, we use these designations for convenience sake only. The first statement, which always contains a complex sequence (in this case *if P, then Q*), we call the *major* premise and it is stated first. The second, categorical premise, we call the *minor* premise and it is stated second.

_____ **The Premises in a Conditional Syllogism.** In a conditional syllogism, like the one used on the previous page, the major premise is a conditional (if ... then) statement. Conditional propositions contain two elements: an *antecedent* and a *consequent*.

Simply stated, the *antecedent* is the part of the complex proposition that comes after the *if*. It is the proposition that provides the *ground* or *logical reason* for the consequent. The *consequent* is the part of the complex proposition that comes after the *then*. It is the proposition which *logically follows* from the antecedent.

In the statement,

If Christ rose from the dead, then Christ is God

the antecedent is *Christ rose from the dead*, and the consequent is *Christ is God*.

This statement, which is the major premise in this argument, is, as we said, a complex statement because it contains two elements: the antecedent and the consequent. The minor premise, however:

When we refer to *terms* in the context of hypothetical syllogisms, we are really referring to whole propositions which we represent by the letters P, Q, etc.

> Christ rose from the dead

does not contain two elements, but only one. It is a categorical statement affirming or denying one of the elements of the major premise (either the antecedent or the consequent). In conditional syllogisms, it is placed second and called the minor premise.

_____ **Two Valid moods.** Conditional syllogisms can be divided into two valid moods. One is called **constructive** and the other is called **destructive**. There are Latin names for both of these. The constructive syllogism is called **modus ponens** (Latin for **affirmative mood**); the destructive syllogism is called **modus tollens** (Latin for **mood of denial**).

In a **constructive** conditional syllogism (**modus ponens**), the minor premise **affirms** the antecedent of the major premise. Constructive syllogisms are always in the following form:

> If P, then Q
> P
> Therefore, Q

The first premise says that, if P is true, then Q must also be true. The second premise says that P, the antecedent, is, in fact, true. It affirms the antecedent P. Therefore, we must conclude, Q is also true.

To go back to our example:

> If Christ rose from the dead, then Christ is God
> Christ rose from the dead
> Therefore, Christ is God

If the proposition **Christ rose from the dead** is true, then the proposition **Christ is God** must also be true. The second premise says that **Christ rose from the dead** is, in fact, true. Therefore, according to the conclusion, **Christ is God** is also true.

A destructive conditional syllogism, which we called **modus tollens**, involves denying the consequent. Destructive syllogisms are always in the following form:

> If P, then Q
> Not Q
> Therefore, not P

The major premise says that if P is true, then Q must also be true. The minor premise says that Q is **not** true. It **denies** the consequent Q. Therefore, we must conclude, P is **not** true.

An example would be:

> If Socrates rose from the dead, then Socrates is God
> Socrates is not God
> Therefore, Socrates did not rise from the dead

In a constructive syllogism, the minor premise affirms the antecedent of the major premise.

The major premise says that if **Socrates rose from the dead** is true, then **Socrates is God** must also be true. The minor premise states that **Socrates is God** is not, in fact, true. It denies that Socrates is God. Therefore, we must conclude, **Socrates rose from the dead** is not true.

Again, as in all formal logic, we say that the **form** of the arguments above are valid. But the **truth of the conclusion** depends upon the truth of the premises.

The two valid moods of conditional syllogisms, then, are: 1) **modus ponens**, **the mood of affirmation**, in which the **antecedent** of the major premise is affirmed, and 2) **modus tollens**, **the mood of denial** in which the **consequent** is denied.

_____ **Two Fallacious Moods.** The two rules above speak of **affirming the antecedent** and **denying the consequent**, but what about the other two possible moods? What about **affirming the consequent** and **denying the antecedent**? Are these moods valid as well?

Asking this question shows that there are, in all, four moods of conditional syllogisms. They are as follows:

Mood #1: affirming the antecedent
Mood #2: denying the consequent
Mood #3: affirming the consequent
Mood #4: denying the antecedent

The first two we know to be valid, but the second two are not. When we try to perform either #3 or #4, we are said to commit a fallacy. The first fallacy (#3) is called the **Fallacy of Affirming the Consequent**. The second (#4) is called the **Fallacy of Denying the Antecedent**.

In fact, if a conditional statement really represents a valid sequence (in other words, if the antecedent really is the ground or reason for the consequent) and the antecedent is true, then the consequent must also be true. But if the antecedent is false, then we cannot say anything about the truth of the consequent: it may either be true or false.

_____ **The Fallacy of Affirming the Consequent.** Let's take a look back at a fallacious form of our example syllogism:

If Christ rose from the dead, then Christ is God
Christ is God
Therefore, Christ rose from the dead

In the example above, we are told, in the major premise, that, if Christ rose from the dead, then Christ is God. Consequently, if the antecedent is true, the consequent must also be true. But when we affirm the consequent (rather than the antecedent), it does not follow that the antecedent is true. From saying, "If it is raining, I will get wet," the statement, "If I get wet, then it is raining" does not logically follow.

The two valid moods of conditional syllogisms are *modus ponens* and *modus tollens*.

The major premise in this syllogism is a conditional statement. Affirming its consequent means we are saying that the consequent is true. But just because the consequent is true, it does not follow that the antecedent is true (which is what we are saying in the conclusion above).

In fact, we could think of a case in which Christ was God, but had not risen from the dead. Let's go back in a time machine to, say, 20 A.D., some time before the crucifixion and resurrection are supposed to have happened. Was Christ God? If we are Christians, we would say, Yes. He was still (even though in earthly form) God the Son, the second person of the Trinity. Had he been resurrected from the dead? We would say, No, not yet. So Christ was God, and, at the same time, He had not risen from the dead.

Therefore, the premises of the above syllogism could be true and the conclusion false, meaning that the syllogism is invalid.

_____ The Fallacy of Denying the Antecedent. Here is the other fallacious form of our example syllogism:

> If Christ rose from the dead, then Christ is God
> Christ did not rise from the dead
> Therefore, Christ is not God

Just because the antecedent is false (the claim of the second premise), it does not follow that the consequent is false (the claim of the conclusion).

Let's say we're still back in 20 A. D. We would say that if Christ rose from the dead, then he was God. But Christ still hadn't risen from the dead, and yet he was still God. Therefore, the first premise would still be true, the second premise true and the conclusion false. The argument is therefore invalid.

_____ Pure Conditional Syllogisms. In all of the conditional syllogisms we have studied so far, the major premise is a conditional statement and the minor premise is a categorical statement. This kind of syllogism is more properly called a **mixed** conditional syllogism because it mixes a conditional statement with a non-conditional statement. There is another kind of conditional syllogism, however. It is called a **pure** conditional syllogism.

In a pure conditional syllogism, **both premises are conditional statements**. They take the following form:

> If Christ is God, then we should follow Him
> If Christ rose from the dead, then Christ is God
> Therefore, If Christ rose from the dead, then we should follow Him

Notice here that the form of a pure hypothetical syllogism is similar to that of a First Figure categorical syllogism, in that the statements are in the same places as the terms of a categorical syllogism:

There is another kind of conditional syllogism called a *pure* conditional syllogism.

If P, then Q
If R, then P
Therefore, If R, then Q

Here you see that P is in the same place as the middle term; R is in the same place as the minor term; and Q in the same place as the major term. Also note that this is pure conditional syllogism in which the antecedent of the minor premise is affirmed in the conclusion. It is therefore an example of *modus ponens*. Pure conditional syllogisms can also be found, however, in *modus tollens*:

If R, then P
If P, then Q
Therefore, If not Q, then not R

In both *modus ponens* and *modus tollens*, the affirmation or denial is passed through the middle term (P in this case). The same rules apply to the pure conditional as apply to mixed conditionals.

_____ **Summary.** In this chapter, we turn from the consideration of categorical syllogisms to the consideration of hypothetical syllogisms. Categorical syllogisms study the relationship between terms; hypothetical syllogisms study the relationships between propositions.

A hypothetical syllogism is a syllogism the first premise of which is a complex, sequential proposition, one member of which is affirmed or denied in the second premise, and the other member of which is consequently affirmed or denied in the conclusion.

There are three kinds of hypothetical syllogisms. They are as follows:

✓ The conditional
✓ The disjunctive
✓ The conjunctive

A conditional syllogism is a syllogism that contains a conditional statement as its major premise, a categorical statement affirming or denying a part of the conditional statement as its minor premise and a categorical statement affirming or denying a part of the major premise as a conclusion.

There are four moods of conditional syllogisms:

Mood #1: affirming the antecedent (*modus ponens*)
Mood #2: denying the consequent (*modus tollens*)
Mood #3: affirming the consequent (*Fallacy of Affirming the Consequent*)
Mood #4: denying the antecedent (*Fallacy of Denying the Antecedent*)

The first two are valid moods and the second two are fallacies.

There are also what are called **pure** conditional syllogisms, in which both premises and the conclusion are conditional statements.

> **T**here are three kinds of hypothetical syllogisms: conditional, disjunctive and conjunctive.

Conditional Syllogisms

Mood	Form	Logical Status
Affirming the Antecedent *Modus Ponens*	If P, then Q P Therefore Q	**Valid**
Denying the Consequent *Modus Tollens*	If P, then Q Not Q Therefore, Not P	**Valid**
Affirming the Consequent *Fallacy of Affirming the Consequent*	If P, then Q Q Therefore P	**Invalid**
Denying the Antecedent *Fallacy of Denying the Antecedent*	If P, then Q Not P Therefore, Not Q	**Invalid**

Pure Conditional Syllogisms:

Modus Ponens:
If P, then Q
If R, then P
Therefore, If R, then Q

Modus Tollens:
If R, then P
If P, then Q
Therefore, If not Q, then not R

_____ **Exercises for Day 1.** **Peruse entire chapter. Then read the introductory section at the very beginning of the chapter. Read this section carefully and try to understand it as best you can.**

1. Until this chapter, what kind of syllogisms have we been studying?

2. Upon what does the validity of categorical syllogisms depend?

3. Upon what does the validity of hypothetical syllogisms depend?

4. Give a brief explanation of categorical reasoning.

5. Give a brief explanation of hypothetical reasoning.

Read section titled, "Types of Hypothetical Syllogisms." Read it carefully.

6. List the three kinds of hypothetical syllogisms.

Read section titled, "Conditional Syllogisms." Read it carefully.

7. Give the definition of a conditional syllogism.

8. Create a conditional syllogism of your own.

Read subsection titled, "A Note on Notation" Read it carefully.

9. Using the new notation outlined in this section, show the form of the syllogism you created in question 8.

Read subsection titled, "Terms and Premises in Hypothetical Syllogisms." Read it carefully.

10. In what way is the word **term** used differently in hypothetical reasoning than in categorical reasoning?

11. In what way are the phrases **major premise** and **minor premise** used differently in the context of hypothetical syllogisms than in the context of categorical syllogisms?

Read subsection titled, "The Major Premise in a Conditional Syllogism." Read it carefully.

12. How is the major premise in a conditional syllogism constructed?

13. How is the minor premise constructed?

14. Define the terms **antecedent** and **consequent**.

15. Identify the antecedent and the consequent in the following conditional statements. (You will need to use the rules of interpreting ordinary language statements to do some of these.)

"If ye were of the world, the world would love his own." (John 15:19)
"...whatsoever is not of faith is sin." (Romans 14:23)
"if any man eat of this bread, he shall live for ever." (John 6:51)

"For if I do this thing willingly, I have a reward ... " (I Corinthians 9:17)
"...if there had been a law given which could have given life, verily righteousness should have been by the law." (Gal. 3:21)
"...whosoever doeth not righteousness is not of God." (I John 3:10)
"And if we know that he hear us, whatsoever we ask, we know that we have the petitions that we desired of him." (I John 5:15)

_____ **Exercises for Day 2.** **Read the section titled, "Two Valid Moods". Read the entire section carefully.**

16. Explain the two valid moods of conditional syllogisms.

17. What is the meaning of **modus ponens** and why is it an appropriate label for the first valid mood?

18. What is the meaning of **modus tollens** and why is it an appropriate label for the second valid mood?

19. Give the form of a **modus ponens** syllogism (use the letters P and Q).

20. Give the form of a **modus tollens** syllogism (use the letters P and Q).

21. Formulate three different **modus ponens** syllogisms.

22. Formulate three different **modus tollens** syllogisms.

Read section titled, "Two Fallacious Moods." Read it carefully.

23. Explain the **Fallacy of Affirming the Consequent**.

24. Explain the **Fallacy of Denying the Antecedent**.

_____ **Exercises for Day 3.** **Read section titled, "The Fallacy of Affirming the Consequent." Read the entire section carefully.**

25. Explain why a conditional syllogism in which the consequent is affirmed is fallacious.

26. Formulate three conditional syllogisms of your own in which the **Fallacy of Affirming the Consequent** is committed.

Read section titled, "The Fallacy of Denying the Antecedent." Read the entire section carefully.

27. Explain why a conditional syllogism in which the antecedent is denied is fallacious.

28. Formulate three conditional syllogisms of your own in which the Fallacy of **Denying the Antecedent** is committed.

29. Tell whether the following syllogisms are valid or invalid by indicating which of the four kinds of conditional syllogisms each is an example of:

If Bilbo puts on the Ring of Power, he becomes invisible
Bilbo puts on the Ring
Therefore, Bilbo becomes invisible

If Frodo reaches Mordor, he can destroy the Ring
Frodo reaches Mordor
Therefore, Frodo can destroy the Ring

If Bilbo puts on the Ring of Power, he becomes invisible
Bilbo does not put on the Ring
Therefore, Bilbo does not become invisible

If Frodo reaches Mordor, he can destroy the Ring
Frodo can destroy the Ring
Therefore, Frodo reaches Mordor

If Bilbo puts on the Ring of Power, he becomes invisible
Bilbo does not become invisible
Therefore, Bilbo has not put on the Ring

If Frodo reaches Mordor, he can destroy the Ring
Frodo does not reach Mordor
Therefore, Frodo does not destroy the Ring

If Bilbo puts on the Ring of Power, he becomes invisible
Bilbo becomes invisible
Therefore, Bilbo has put on the Ring

If Frodo reaches Mordor, he can destroy the Ring
Frodo cannot destroy the Ring
Therefore, Frodo does not reach Mordor

30. Do the following in each of the following arguments:

   1) **Write out the form of the argument using *P*'s and *Q*'s, supplying any missing premises if it is an enthymeme.**
   2) **Indicate which mood the syllogism is in.**
   3) **Indicate whether the syllogism is valid or invalid and why.**
   4) **Change each invalid syllogism to a valid one by changing either element of the major premise or the entire minor premise from affirmative to negative or vice-versa.**

If abortion kills an innocent human being, then abortion is wrong. Therefore, abortion is wrong.

If Americans recognize that we have lost our moral bearings, there might be hope for our country. But most Americans have not realized the problem. Therefore, there is no hope for our country.

If we give trade privileges to countries that violate human rights, we will only encourage them to continue to violate them. Unfortunately we are continuing to grant such privileges to countries like China.

If we don't stop developers who profit from urban sprawl, then we will destroy what little green space we have left. But we're doing little to stop them.

If religious authority resides in the church, then it does not reside in the Bible. But religious authority does not reside in the church; therefore, it must reside in the Bible

If public schools really reflect the values of their communities, then they will allow school prayer. But we all know that public schools do not really reflect the values of their communities. And that's why they do not allow school prayer.

If we are descended from animals, then we must treat them as we treat human beings. But we are not descended from animals. Therefore, we are not obligated to treat them as we treat humans.

If America becomes a secular nation, then we will ultimately lose our sense of morality. But America is not yet a secular nation. Therefore, we have not yet lost our sense of morality.

If the government takes over the health care industry, the quality of medical care will deteriorate. Fortunately, attempts by government to take over the health care industry in recent years have been turned back, and the quality of medical care has not deteriorated.

If you are saved by faith, then you are not saved by works. We are saved by faith. Therefore, we are not saved by works.

If poverty causes crime, then crime rates should be high when poverty rates are high and low when poverty rates are low. But crime rates are not high when poverty rates are high and low when poverty rates are low. Therefore, we know that poverty does not cause crime.

_____ **Exercises for Day 4.** **Read section titled, "Pure Conditional Syllogisms." Read it carefully.**

31. What differentiates pure conditional syllogisms from mixed conditionals?

32. Give the form of a pure conditional syllogism.

33. Give the form of the following pure conditional syllogisms using the indicated letters:

> If we are truly to have freedom of speech, then there can be no censorship. And if there is no censorship, then there will be a freer exchange of ideas. Therefore, if we are truly to have freedom of speech, there will be a freer exchange of ideas. (F, C, E)

> If illegal immigration continues unchecked, American civilization will be destroyed. And if American civilization is destroyed, the last, best hope for freedom will have been extinguished. Therefore, if illegal immigration continues, the last best hope of freedom will have been extinguished. (I, A, H)

> If we do not return to fair trade practices which protect small family businesses, then our local economies will be destroyed. And if our local economies are destroyed, then local culture will eventually become extinct. Therefore if we do not return to fair trade practices which protect small family businesses, then local culture will eventually become extinct. (F, E, C)

34. Formulate your own examples of each of the four moods of conditional syllogisms.

Read section titled, "Summary." Read it carefully.

35. Indicate whether the following are true or false:

T	F	There are four valid moods of conditional syllogisms.
T	F	One of the invalid moods is called the *Fallacy of Affirming the Antecedent*.
T	F	A conditional syllogism and a conjunctive syllogism are both hypothetical syllogisms.
T	F	The major premise in a hypothetical syllogism is the premise which contains the major term.
T	F	The consequent is the proposition in a conditional statement that appears before the *then*.

_____ **Weekly Analysis Assignment.** **Find an article from a newspaper (letters to the editor in newspapers are ideal) or magazine or a chapter from a book you are reading that contains conditional reasoning. Either write a short 1-2 page essay or make a presentation in class analyzing the argument. The paper or presentation should contain the following elements:**

1. A *presentation* of the argument as it was originally written.
2. A *summary* of the argument in your own words.
3. An *analysis* of the logical form of the argument.
4. An *evaluation* of the argument's soundness. This will involve assessing both the truth of the argument's premises and its validity. Remember that if the argument is valid and the premises are true, the conclusion must be true. If the argument is valid and one or more of the premises are false, then the conclusion must also be false. And if the argument is invalid, the truth of the conclusion cannot be determined one way or another by knowing the truth of the premises.
5. State your agreement or disagreement with the argument you have analyzed.

PLATO

The Power of Love

_____The Argument in Plain Language: "People don't appreciate what love really is."

_____The Argument: "Mankind, he said, judging from their neglect of him, have never, as I think, at all understood the power of Love. For if they had understood Him they would surely have built noble temples and altars, and offer solemn sacrifices in His honor; but this is not done."
—**Plato, *Symposium***

_____Background of the Argument: The *Symposium* is thought to be one of, if not the greatest of Plato's dialogues, possibly as great as the *Republic*. The setting is a dinner party discussion at which Socrates is a guest. Agathon, a poet, begins to speak about human love. This prompts Socrates, the protagonist in all of Plato's dialogues, to launch into a discourse on love, but less on a human level than a divine one. He argues that by loving beautiful people, we go on to love, not the beauty we see, but the beauty we do not see. From there we go on to love beautiful ideas and thoughts, until, eventually, we begin to love Beauty itself. In so doing, we become closer to God. Some of the passages in the *Symposium* are reminiscent of the passages on love in *I Corinthians* 13, indicating that the Greeks, through the general revelation Paul discusses in *Romans*, had been able to apprehend dimly some of the truths that would later be revealed more fully after the coming of Christ.

_____Assignment:
1. Try to put the argument in the form of a syllogism.
2. Write a short 1-2 page essay explaining why you think the argument is sound or unsound. If you think it is unsound, offer your argument for why you think this. This will involve an assessment also of whether the premises are true. Give reasons for your position.
3. Write a short 2-3 page biographical essay on Plato.

> "Since it is Reason which shapes and regulates all other things, it ought not itself to be left in disorder."
>
> —**Epectetus**

Hypothetical Syllogisms

Disjunctive Syllogisms

_____ **What is a Disjunctive Syllogism?** In the last chapter, we discussed the first of the three kinds of hypothetical syllogisms: the *conditional* syllogism. In this chapter, we will discuss the second of the three kinds of hypothetical syllogisms: the *disjunctive* syllogism.

In a conditional syllogism, the major premise is a conditional proposition (an *if ... then* statement) and the minor premise is a categorical statement (an A, E, I or 0 statement) that affirms or denies one of the simple propositions that make up the major premise. In a disjunctive syllogism, the major premise is a *disjunctive* proposition and the minor premise is a categorical proposition that either affirms or denies one of the alternants in the major premise.

_____ **The Elements of a Disjunctive Proposition.** In order to understand how a disjunctive syllogism works, we must first have an understanding of the disjunctive statement. A disjunctive statement is an *either ... or* statement. Let's look at an example:

> Either Jesus is a man or Jesus is God

The disjunctive proposition is made up of two elements (both of which are simple categorical propositions). The two elements are called *alternants*. There is the first alternant and the second alternant. To put it simply, the first alternant is the proposition before the *or*, and the second is the proposition after the *or*.

For example, in the statement:

> Either Islam is true or Christianity is true

the first alternant is ***Islam is true***. The second alternant is ***Christianity is true***.

> **A** disjunctive statement is an *either ... or* statement.

Disjunctive statements take the following form:

Either P or Q

We call a hypothetical syllogism a disjunctive syllogism when its major premise is a disjunctive statement. The following is an example:

Either Islam is true or Christianity is true
Islam is not true
Therefore, Christianity is true

_____ **Disjunctive Moods.** Disjunctive syllogisms can involve either denying one of the alternants (thereby affirming the other alternant in the conclusion), in which case they are said to be ***tollendo ponens*** (Latin for affirmation by denial), or they may involve affirming one of the alternants (thereby denying the other alternant) and are said to be ***ponendo tollens*** (Latin for denial by affirmation). There are two moods under *tollendo ponens*, one of which involves denying the first alternant (affirming the second), and the other denying the second alternant (affirming the first). Likewise, there are two moods under *ponendo tollens*, one of which involves affirming the first alternant (denying the second) and the other affirming the second alternant (denying the first).

Altogether then, the moods are as follows:

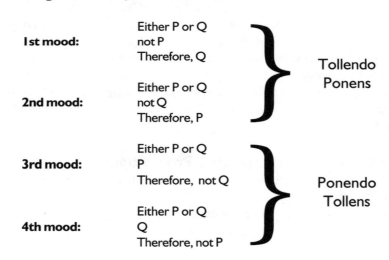

The first two moods, both of which are *tollendo ponens*, are valid, while the second two moods, both of which are *ponendo tollens*, are invalid.

_____ **Valid Disjunctive Moods.** There are two valid disjunctive moods. The first two moods, both of which are ***tollendo ponens***, are valid, while the second two moods, both of which ***ponendo tollens***, are invalid. In other words, disjunctive syllogisms are valid when they affirm by denying, but are not valid when they deny by affirming.

The first invalid mood we refer to as The ***Fallacy of Affirming the First Alternant***, and the second as the ***Fallacy of Affirming the Second Alternant***.

Let's look at an example of each of the disjunctive moods:

1st valid mood:	Either Socrates is a farmer or Socrates is a philosopher Socrates is not a farmer Therefore, Socrates is a philosopher
2nd valid mood:	Either Socrates is a farmer or Socrates is a philosopher Socrates is not a philosopher Therefore, Socrates is a farmer
Fallacy of Affirming First Alternant:	Either Jesus is God or Jesus is a man Jesus is God Therefore, Jesus is not a man
Fallacy of Affirming Second Alternant:	Either Jesus is God or Jesus is a man Jesus is a man Therefore, Jesus is not God

Disjunctive syllogisms are valid when they affirm by denying, but are not valid when they deny by affirming.

The first two moods are considered valid because we are told in the major premise that at least one of the alternants must be true. If one of the alternants is false, we know, therefore, that the other must be true. We know the second two moods to be invalid since, from saying that one alternant is true (which is what the minor premise asserts), we cannot conclude the other is false. They may both be true.

In the example above, we can certainly conceive of a case in which someone could be both a farmer and a philosopher. In which case, affirming that Socrates is a philosopher does not necessarily mean that he is not a farmer.

There is one case, however, in which all four moods would be considered valid. This occurs when the disjuncts are contradictory to one another. In this case, not only does the falsehood of one imply the truth of the other, but the truth of one implies the falsehood of the other. This is because only one **but not both** of the disjuncts in an exclusive disjunction can be true at the same time.

A note on exclusive and inclusive disjunctions: We should also point out that there are two kinds of disjunctive statements. The first is called an **exclusive** disjunction. The second is called an **inclusive** disjunction.

An **exclusive** disjunction is a disjunctive statement in which **only one of the alternants can be true, but not both**. You know that a disjunctive statement is an exclusive disjunction when you see that the alternants in the disjunctive statement are contradictory. The form of an exclusive disjunction is as follows:

Either P or not P

An example of an exclusive disjunction would be as follows:

Either Christianity is true or Christianity is not true

This proposition is an exclusive disjunction because the first alternant **Christianity is true** is contradictory to **Christianity is not true**. Only one of these alternants may be true, but not both—Christianity cannot be true and untrue at the same time.

An *inclusive* disjunction is a disjunctive statement in which **one or both** of the alternants can be true. An example would be:

Either God is spiritual or angels are spiritual

Since the two alternants are not contradictory, this is an *inclusive* disjunction, since both could be true at the same time (and in fact are).

An illustration which might make this clearer is the warning sometimes seen for rides at an amusement park: 'If you have a heart condition or you are pregnant, you may not ride on this attraction.' This sign is telling you that if **either one or both** of the conditions apply, then the warning should be heeded. It is obviously an inclusive disjunction. If it were exclusive, then the statement would have to be considered false—and people who were both suffering from heart conditions and pregnant could go on the ride!

Unless otherwise indicated (or unless the alternants are clearly contradictory), disjunctive statements should be considered *inclusive* disjunctions.

_____ **Reduction of Disjunctive Syllogisms to Conditional Syllogisms.** You will remember that in previous chapters we learned how to reduce Second, Third and Fourth Figure categorical syllogisms to the First Figure. We did this because the validity of a syllogism is more obvious in the First Figure. For the same reason, it is sometimes useful to reduce disjunctive syllogisms to conditional syllogisms, since validity is more obvious in conditional syllogisms than in other kinds of hypothetical arguments. Disjunctive syllogisms can be reduced to conditional syllogisms as follows:

Either Socrates is a farmer or Socrates is a philosopher
Socrates is not a farmer
Therefore, Socrates is a philosopher

BECOMES

If Socrates is a not a philosopher, then Socrates is a farmer
Socrates is not a farmer
Therefore, Socrates is a philosopher

This is done by observing the following rules:

Rule #1: The minor premise and the conclusion must remain unchanged
Rule #2: The major premise is changed from a disjunctive statement to a conditional statement by:
　Step #1: Placing the disjunct denied in the minor premise in the place of the consequent; and
　Step #2: Placing the denial of the other conjunct in the place of the antecedent

We say that the first invalid mood commits the *Fallacy of Affirming the First Alternant* and that the second invalid mood commits the *Fallacy of Affirming the Second Alternant.*

_____ **Summary.** In a disjunctive syllogism, the major premise is a ***disjunctive*** proposition and the minor premise is a categorical proposition that either affirms or denies one of the alternatives in the major premise. A disjunctive statement is an ***either ... or*** statement.

Disjunctive syllogisms are divided into four different moods, two of which (as with conditional syllogisms) are valid and two of which are invalid. Disjunctive syllogisms affirm by denying. The disjunctive proposition is made up of two elements (both of which are simple categorical propositions). The two elements are called ***alternants***. The first alternant is the proposition before the ***or***, and the second is the proposition after the ***or***.

There are two valid disjunctive moods. Both involve ***tollendo ponens***, affirming by denying. The first involves denying the first alternant, thereby affirming the second alternant. The second involves denying the second alternant, thereby affirming the first alternant.

The two invalid moods are examples of ***ponendo tollens***, denying by affirming. We say that syllogisms in the first invalid mood commits the ***Fallacy of Affirming the First Alternant***. We say that syllogisms in the second invalid mood commit the ***Fallacy of Affirming the Second Alternant***.

In addition, we said that there are two kinds of disjunctive statements: ***inclusive*** and ***exclusive***. Which kind of disjunction (inclusive or exclusive) is used in the major premise of a disjunctive syllogism will also affect whether the last two moods are valid. If the major premise is an ***inclusive*** disjunction, then the last two moods are invalid. If it is an ***exclusive*** disjunction, then the last two moods are valid.

The general rule is: the statement is to be considered inclusive ***unless*** it is a contradiction or if it is clearly an exclusive disjunction.

Disjunctive Syllogisms

Mood	**Form**	**Logical Status**
Denying the First Alternant	Either P or Q Not P Therefore Q	**Valid**
Denying the Second Alternant	Either P or Q Not Q Therefore, P	**Valid**
Affirming the First Alternant	Either P or Q P Therefore, not P	**Invalid**
Affirming the Second Alternant	Either P or Q Q Therefore, Not P	**Invalid**

Tollendo
Ponens

Ponendo
Tollens

Inclusive vs. Exclusive Disjunctions*:

Inclusive Disjunction: Either P or Q

Exclusive Disjunction: Either P or not P

*Note that the logical status of the four moods above assumes that the major premise is an inclusive disjunction. For disjunctive syllogisms in which the major premise is an exclusive disjunction, however, all moods are considered valid.

_____ **Exercises for Day I.** **Peruse entire chapter. Then read section titled, "What is a Disjunctive Syllogism?" Read this section carefully and try to understand it as best you can.**

1. Name the three types of hypothetical syllogisms. [Review]

2. Give the definition of a disjunctive syllogism.

3. In a disjunctive syllogism, what kind of proposition is the major premise?

4. In a disjunctive syllogism, what kind of proposition is the minor premise?

Read section titled, "The Elements of a Disjunctive Proposition." Read it carefully.

5. What is a disjunctive statement?

6. Give the form of disjunctive statements. (use **P** and **Q**)

7. Give an example of a disjunctive statement that is different from the ones found in the book.

8. What do we call the elements of a disjunctive statement?

9. How many of them are there?

10. Where do you find the first alternant?

11. Where do you find the second alternant?

12. What is the first alternant in the disjunctive proposition you wrote in answer to question 7 above?

13. What is the second alternant in the disjunctive proposition you wrote in answer to question 7 above?

_____ **Exercises for Day 2.** **Read sections titled, "Disjunctive Moods" and "Valid Disjunctive Moods." Read them carefully.**

14. How many of the four possible moods for disjunctive syllogisms are valid?

15. What Latin phrase do we use to characterize valid disjunctive moods? What does it mean in English?

16. What Latin phrase do we use to characterize the invalid disjunctive moods? What does it mean in English?

17. Give the form of a syllogism in the first valid mood. (use **P** and **Q**)

18. Create a disjunctive syllogism in the first valid disjunctive mood.

19. Give the form of a syllogism in the second valid disjunctive mood. (use **P** and **Q**)

20. Create a disjunctive syllogism in the second valid disjunctive mood.

21. Give the form of a syllogism in the first invalid mood. (use **P** and **Q**)

22. Create a disjunctive syllogism in the first invalid disjunctive mood.

23. Give the form of a syllogism in the second invalid mood. (use **P** and **Q**)

24. Create a disjunctive syllogism in the second invalid disjunctive mood.

25. Do the following in each of the following syllogisms:

    1) Write out the form of the argument using *P*'s and *Q*'s.
    2) Indicate the mood of the syllogism.
    3) Indicate whether the syllogism is valid or invalid and why.
    4) Change each invalid syllogism to a valid one by changing either element of the major premise or the entire minor premise from affirmative to negative or vice-versa.

    Example: Either Socrates is a farmer or Socrates is a philosopher
                    Socrates is a farmer
                    Therefore, Socrates is not a philosopher

    1)   Either P or Q   2) First invalid mood (Fallacy of Affirming the First Alternant)
                P   3) Invalid (since it is *ponendo tollens* rather than *tollendo ponens* OR since the syllogism
                Therefore, not Q   denies by affirming rather than affirming by denying)

    4)   Either Socrates is a farmer or Socrates is a philosopher
                Socrates is not a farmer
                Therefore, Socrates is a philosopher

                    (the syllogism is now of the following form: Either P or Q
                                                            not P
                                                        Therefore, Q
                which is *tollendo ponens*. And since all disjunctive syllogisms that are *tollendo ponens* are valid (since they affirm by denying) it is now a valid syllogism.

Either Frodo destroys the Ring or evil will triumph   Either Bilbo solves the riddle or Gollum will eat him
Frodo destroys the Ring   Gollum will not eat him
Therefore, evil will not triumph   Therefore, Bilbo solves the riddle

Either Frodo destroys the Ring or evil will triumph   Either Bilbo solves the riddle or Gollum will eat him
Evil will not triumph   Bilbo solves the riddle
Therefore, Frodo destroys the Ring   Therefore, Gollum will not eat him

Either Frodo destroys the Ring or evil will triumph   Either Bilbo solves the riddle or Gollum will eat him
Evil will triumph   Bilbo does not solve the riddle
Therefore, Frodo does not destroy the Ring   Therefore, Gollum will eat him

Either Frodo destroys the Ring or evil will triumph   Either Bilbo solves the riddle or Gollum will eat him
Frodo does not destroy the Ring   Gollum will eat him
Therefore, evil will triumph   Therefore, Bilbo does not solve the riddle

_____ **Exercises for Day 3.**

Read subsection titled, "A Note on Inclusive and Exclusive Disjunctions." Read it carefully.

26. What are the two kinds of disjunctive statements?

27. What is an exclusive disjunction?

28. Using P and Q to stand for the disjuncts, give the form of an exclusive disjunctive statement.

29. Give an example of an exclusive disjunctive proposition not found in the book.

30. What relationship of opposition (you can look back to Chapter 6 of Book I if you need help) characterizes the alternants in exclusive disjunctions?

31. What is an inclusive disjunction?

32. Using P and Q to stand for the disjuncts, give the form of an inclusive disjunctive statement.

33. Give an example of an inclusive disjunctive proposition not found in the book.

34. How do you determine whether a disjunctive statement is inclusive or exclusive?

35. Under what condition could the invalid disjunctive moods be considered valid?

Read section titled, "Reduction of Disjunctive Syllogisms to Conditional Syllogisms." Read the entire section carefully.

36. Reduce the valid syllogisms in question 25 to conditional syllogisms.

37. Do the following in each of the following arguments:

   1) **Write out the form of the argument using *P*'s and *Q*'s, supplying any missing premises if it is an enthymeme.**
   2) **Indicate which mood the syllogism is in.**
   3) **Indicate whether the syllogism is valid or invalid and why.**
   4) **Change each invalid syllogism to a valid one by changing either element of the major premise or the entire minor premise from affirmative to negative or vice-versa.**

   Abortion destroys a human fetus, which is either a human being or a mass of tissue. But we know that the fetus is not just a mass of tissue. Therefore, abortion destroys a human being.

   Either we stop developers who profit from urban sprawl or they will destroy what little green space we have left. Unfortunately, we are doing little to stop them.

   America is either a secular nation or a Christian one. We know it's not a secular one, so it must be a Christian one.

   We can either give trade privileges to countries that violate human rights or we can uphold the cause of freedom and democracy around the world. Those are our choices. Unfortunately we have given trade privileges to countries like China.

   Religious authority resides in either the Bible or the Church. Catholics believe it resides in the Church. Therefore, they do not believe that it resides in the Bible.

Either we continue to protect the rights of gun owners or we violate the Second Amendment to the Constitution. We do not violate the Second Amendment. Therefore, we continue to protect the rights of gun owners.

Either we allow prayer in public schools or we disregard the wishes of most parents. But we do not allow prayer in public schools. Therefore, we are disregarding the wishes of most parents.

Either intermediate life forms will be found in the fossil record or the theory of evolution will decline in influence. But we are still not finding these intermediate forms. Therefore, the theory of evolution will decline in influence.

You are saved either by faith or by works. We are saved by faith. Therefore, we are not saved by works.

Developed countries must either give up their attachment to socialism or their economies will continue to languish. Unfortunately, many of them continue to practice socialism, leaving their economies in tatters.

We can either continue to hand out checks to welfare recipients or make them go to work. With welfare reform, we have stopped handing out checks to welfare recipients and are making them go back to work.

We will either have freedom of speech or censorship. We have censorship. Therefore, we cannot have free speech.

Either we must return to fair trade practices which protected small family businesses or our local economies will be destroyed. Our local economies are being destroyed. Therefore, we must not have returned to fair trade practices.

Either illegal immigration will continue unchecked or American civilization will be preserved. Realistically, however, there is no way to prevent this invasion of our borders.

Either we do something or the size of government will continue to grow. Yet little is being done. Therefore, the size of government will continue to grow.

_____ Exercises for Day 4. **Read section titled, "Summary." Read the entire section carefully.**

38. Formulate a disjunctive syllogism of your own which is invalid because it commits the *Fallacy of Affirming the First Alternant*.

39. Formulate a disjunctive syllogism of your own which is invalid because it commits the *Fallacy of Affirming the Second Alternant*.

40. Formulate two of your own examples for each of the four moods of the Second Figure.

41. Indicate whether the following are true or false:

T	F	There are four valid moods of disjunctive syllogisms.
T	F	The invalid moods are all *tollendo ponens*.
T	F	A conditional syllogism and a disjunctive syllogism are both hypothetical syllogisms.
T	F	The major premise in a disjunctive syllogism is the premise which contains the major term.
T	F	The alternant is the proposition of a disjunctive statement that appears only in the conclusion.
T	F	A disjunctive statement in which one alternant is true and the other false is a false statement.

_____ **Weekly Analysis Assignment.** Find an article from a newspaper (letters to the editor in newspapers are ideal) or magazine or a chapter from a book you are reading that contains disjunctive reasoning. Either write a short 1-2 page essay or make a presentation in class analyzing the argument. The paper or presentation should contain the following elements:

1. A **presentation** of the argument as it was originally written.
2. A **summary** of the argument in your own words.
3. An **analysis** of the logical form of the argument.
4. An **evaluation** of the argument's soundness. This will involve assessing both the truth of the argument's premises and its validity. Remember that if the argument is valid and the premises are true, the conclusion must be true. If the argument is valid and one or more of the premises are false, then the conclusion must also be false. And if the argument is invalid, the truth of the conclusion cannot be determined one way or another by knowing the truth of the premises.
5. State your agreement or disagreement with the argument you have analyzed.

C. S. Lewis

The Trilemma: the Deity of Christ

_____**The Argument in Plain Language:** There is no way Jesus can merely be a good man.

_____**The Argument:** "I am trying to prevent anyone saying the really foolish thing that people often say about Him: 'I'm ready to accept Jesus as a great moral teacher, but I don't accept His claim to be God.' That is the one thing we must not say. A man who was merely a man and said the sort of things Jesus said would not be a great moral teacher. He would either be a lunatic—on a level with a man who says he is a poached egg—or else he would be the Devil of Hell. You must make your choice. Either this man was, and is, the Son of God: or else a man or something worse. You can shut Him up for a fool. You can spit at Him and kill Him as a demon, or you can fall at His feet and call Him Lord and God. But let us not come with any patronizing nonsense about His being a great human teacher. He has not left that open to us. He did not intend to."

—C. S. Lewis, *Mere Christianity*

_____**Background of the Argument:** This argument is commonly referred to as "The Trilemma." This title is somewhat deceptive, since it implies that the argument is in the form of a dilemma, but with three horns rather than the standard two (see Chapter 13 on dilemmas). However, the argument is not in the form of a dilemma, but a disjunctive hypothetical syllogism-the only difference being that its major premise contains three disjuncts rather than two (as in the ones we have studied). It is proposed as a proof of the deity of Christ. The argument, indeed, has the most force with the person it is directed at: the person who wants to say that Jesus was a great moral teacher and no more. When Lewis uttered this argument (in a radio talk on the B. B. C. during World War II), this was a very common opinion—and still is. However, with the person who believes that Jesus could be a liar or a lunatic (an opinion that would be quite hard to justify, but still believed by some atheists), the argument has much less force. There is a form of this argument (a quite embryonic form of it) in G. K. Chesterton's *Everlasting Man*, (written in 1927), a book that Lewis cited as a major influence on his thought.

_____**Assignment:**
1. Put the argument in the form of a disjunctive syllogism. The only difference will be that there will be three disjuncts in the major premise and the minor premise will involve the denial of two of the disjuncts rather than just one.
2. Write a short 1-2 page essay explaining why you think the argument is sound or unsound.
3. Write a short 2-3 page biographical essay on C. S. Lewis.

"The decision doesn't have to be logical; it was unanimous"

—Anonymous

Hypothetical Syllogisms

Conjunctive Syllogisms

_____ **What is a Conjunctive Syllogism?** In the last chapter, we discussed the second of the three kinds of hypothetical syllogisms: the *disjunctive* syllogism. In this chapter, we will discuss the third of the three kinds of hypothetical syllogisms: the *conjunctive* syllogism.

In a *conditional* syllogism, the major premise is a *conditional* proposition (an *if ... then* statement) and the minor premise is a categorical statement (an A, E, I or 0 statement) that affirms or denies one of the simple propositions that make up the major premise. In a *disjunctive* syllogism, the major premise is a *disjunctive* proposition (an *either ... or* statement) and the minor premise is a categorical proposition that either affirms or denies one of the alternants in the major premise. In a *conjunctive* syllogism, the major premise is a *conjunctive* proposition (a *both ... and* statement) which denies that the two propositions contained in the major premise can be true at the same time. The minor premise is a categorical statement that affirms or denies one of the simple propositions that make up the major premise.

_____ **The Elements of a Conjunctive Proposition.** In order to understand how a conjunctive syllogism works, let us again try to get an understanding of the kind of statement that is used in the major premise. A *conjunctive* statement is a *both ... and* statement. Let's look at an example:

Jesus is both man and God

The conjunctive proposition is made up of two elements (both of which are simple categorical propositions). The two elements are called *conjuncts*. There is the first conjunct and the second conjunct.

In a conjunctive syllogism, the major premise is a conjunctive proposition which denies that the two propositions contained in the major premise can be true at the same time.

To put it simply, the first conjunct is the proposition before the ***and***, and the second is the proposition after the ***and***.

For example, in the statement:

Islam is true and Christianity is true

the first conjunct is ***Islam is true***. The second conjunct is ***Christianity is true***.

Conjunctive statements take the following form:

Both P and Q

Be aware that the word ***both*** does not have to appear in the statement in order for it to be considered a conjunctive proposition, although it does underscore the fact that both conjuncts must be true in order for the whole statement to be true.

_____ **The Conjunctive Syllogism.** Remember we said in the introduction that in a ***conjunctive*** syllogism, the major premise is a ***conjunctive*** proposition (a ***both ... and*** statement) which ***denies*** that the two propositions contained in the major premise can be true at the same time. The minor premise is a categorical statement that affirms or denies one of the simple propositions that make up the major premise.

In other words, the major premise in a conjunctive syllogism is not just a conjunctive statement, but a ***negated*** conjunctive statement. An example of a conjunctive syllogism is:

Socrates cannot be both a man and a god
Socrates is a man
Therefore, Socrates is not a god

This syllogism takes the following symbolic form:

Not both P and Q
P
Therefore, not Q

_____ **Conjunctive Moods.** The mood of a conjunctive syllogism is determined by whether the minor premise affirms or denies one of the conjuncts. If the minor premise ***affirms*** one of the conjuncts (thereby denying the other in the conclusion), it is called ***ponendo tollens*** (denial by affirmation). If the minor premise ***denies*** one of the conjuncts, it is called ***tollendo ponens*** (affirmation by denial).

As with conditional and disjunctive syllogisms, conjunctive syllogisms are divided into four different moods:

Like conditional and disjunctive syllogisms, conjunctive syllogisms take two valid and two invalid moods.

Affirming the First Conjunct:	Not both P and Q P Therefore, not Q	} Ponendo Tollens
Affirming the Second Conjunct:	Not both P and Q Q Therefore, not P	
Denying the First Conjunct:	Not both P and Q Not P Therefore, Q	} Tollendo Ponens
Denying the Second Conjunct:	Not both P and Q Not Q Therefore, P	

_____ **Valid Conjunctive Moods.** In disjunctive syllogisms, the two valid moods were *tollendo ponens* and the invalid moods were *ponendo tollens.* With conjunctive syllogisms, however, just the reverse is true. All valid moods are *ponendo tollens* and all invalid moods are *tollendo ponens*. In other words, while a disjunctive syllogism must affirm by denying, a conjunctive syllogism must deny by affirming.

Let's look at an example of each of the valid conjunctive moods:

Affirming the First Conjunct:	Socrates cannot be both a farmer and a philosopher Socrates is a farmer Therefore, Socrates is not a philosopher
Affirming the Second Conjunct:	Socrates cannot be both a farmer and a philosopher Socrates is a philosopher Therefore, Socrates is not a farmer
Fallacy of Denying the First Conjunct:	Socrates cannot be both a farmer and a philosopher Socrates is not a farmer Therefore, Socrates is a philosopher
Fallacy of Denying the Second Conjunct:	Socrates cannot be both a farmer and a philosopher Socrates is not a philosopher Therefore, Socrates is a farmer

In each case above, the major premise asserts that both of the conjuncts cannot be true. So we know that at least one of the conjuncts must be false. Notice that, in the valid moods, one conjunct in the major premise is being affirmed in order to deny the other conjunct (*ponendo tollens*.

In the invalid moods, one conjunct in the major premise is denied in order to affirm the other (*tollendo ponens*). These moods are invalid because they assume that if one conjunct is false the other must be true. But the major premise does not state this. It states only that they cannot both be true; it does not state that they cannot both be false. If both conjuncts are false, then denying one of the them does not mean the other is true.

With conjunctive syllogisms, all valid moods deny by affirming (*ponendo tollens*) and all invalid moods affirm by denying (*tollendo ponens*).

Conjunctive syllogisms in which the major premise is a perfect conjunction are valid in all four moods.

A note on Formally Perfect Conjunctions. Once again, as in other types of hypothetical syllogisms, there are circumstances under which invalid moods can be considered valid. In disjunctive syllogisms, this was seen to be the case when the disjuncts in the major premise were *exclusive* disjunctions. Similarly, in conjunctive syllogisms, when the two conjuncts are contradictory propositions (in other words they cannot both be true or both be false at the same time), invalid moods also become valid. When a conjunctive statement is contradictory, we say it is formally perfect.

_____ **Reduction of Conjunctive Syllogisms to Conditional Syllogisms.** Conjunctive syllogisms, like disjunctive syllogisms, can be reduced to conditional syllogisms as follows:

> Socrates cannot be both a philosopher and a farmer
> Socrates is a philosopher
> Therefore, Socrates is not a farmer
>
> BECOMES
>
> If Socrates is a philosopher, then he is not a farmer
> Socrates is a philosopher
> Therefore, Socrates is not a farmer

Notice that the only proposition in the argument that has changed is the major premise. The conjunctive statement in the major premise is changed to an equivalent conditional statement by making one conjunct in the original syllogism the antecedent and the denial of the the other conjunct the consequent. This is done by observing the following rules:

> **Rule #1:** The minor premise and the conclusion must remain unchanged
> **Rule #2:** The major premise is changed from a conjunctive statement to a conditional statement by:
> **Step #1:** Placing the conjunct affirmed in the minor premise in the place of the antecedent; and
> **Step #2:** Placing the denial of the other conjunct in the place of the consequent

_____ **Summary.** In a conjunctive syllogism, the major premise is a negated *conjunctive* proposition and the minor premise is a categorical proposition that either affirms or denies one of the elements of the major premise. A conjunctive statement is a *both ... and* statement.

Conjunctive syllogisms are divided into four moods. All *ponendo tollens* moods are valid and all *tollendo ponens* moods are invalid.

Unlike disjunctive syllogisms, which affirm by denying, conjunctive syllogisms deny by affirming. The conjunctive proposition is made up of two elements (both of which are simple categorical propositions). The two elements are called *conjuncts*. The first conjunct is the proposition before the *and*, and the second is the proposition after the *and*.

When the conjuncts are contradictory, we call the conjunction *formally perfect*. If the major premise in a conjunctive syllogism is formally perfect, it is valid in all four moods.

Conjunctive Syllogisms

Mood	Form	Logical Status
Affirming the First Conjunct	Not both P and Q P Therefore, not Q	**Valid**
Affirming the Second Conjunct	Not both P and Q Q Therefore, not P	**Valid**
Denying the First Conjunct	Not both P and Q Not P Therefore, Q	**Invalid**
Denying the Second Conjunct	Not both P and Q Not Q Therefore, P	**Invalid**

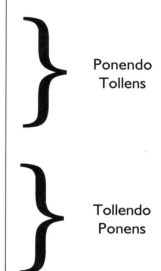

Ponendo Tollens

Tollendo Ponens

Inclusive vs. Exclusive Conjunctions*:

Standard conjunction: Not both P and Q

Formally perfect conjunction: Not both P and not P

*Note that the logical status of the four moods above assumes that the major premise is a standard conjunction (formally imperfect). For conjunctive syllogisms in which the major premise is a formally perfect conjunction, however (in other words, one in which the conjuncts are contradictory to one another), all the moods are considered valid.

_____ **Exercises for Day 1.** **Peruse entire chapter. Then read the section titled, "What is a Conjunctive Syllogism?" Read this section carefully and try to understand it as best you can.**

1. Name the three types of hypothetical syllogisms. [Review]

2. Give the definition of a conjunctive syllogism.

3. In a conjunctive syllogism, what kind of proposition is the major premise?

4. In a conjunctive syllogism, what kind of proposition is the minor premise?

Read section titled, "The Elements of a Conjunctive Proposition." Read it carefully.

5. What is a conjunctive statement?

6. Give the form of conjunctive statements. (Use P and Q)

7. Construct a conjunctive statement different from the examples found in the book.

8. What do we call the **elements** of a conjunctive statement?

9. How many of them are there?

10. Where do you find the first conjunct?

11. Where do you find the second conjunct?

12. What is the first conjunct in the conjunctive proposition you wrote in answer to question 6 above?

13. What is the second conjunct in the conjunctive proposition you wrote in answer to question 6 above?

_____ **Exercises for Day 2.** **Read section titled, "The Conjunctive Syllogism." Read it carefully.**

14. Describe the major premise in a conjunctive syllogism.

15. Describe the minor premise in a conjunctive syllogism.

16. Give the symbolic form of a conjunctive syllogism.

17. Construct your own conjunctive syllogism.

Read sections titled, "Conjunctive Moods" and "Valid Conjunctive Moods." Read them carefully.

18. Tell the number of moods into which conjunctive syllogisms are divided.

19. Give the form of a syllogism in the first valid mood. (Use P and Q)

20. Create a conjunctive syllogism in the first valid conjunctive mood.

21. Give the form of a syllogism in the second valid mood. (Use **P** and **Q**)

22. Create a disjunctive syllogism in the second valid disjunctive mood.

23. Explain in your own words why conjunctive syllogisms that deny by affirming are valid and conjunctive syllogisms that affirm by denying are normally invalid.

Read subsection titled, "A Note on Formally Perfect Conjunctions." Read it carefully.

24. Explain in your own words why conjunctive syllogisms that affirm by denying are normally invalid but are considered valid when the major premise is a formally perfect conjunctive statement.

25. In each of the following syllogisms:

    1) Write out the form of the argument using P's and Q's.
    2) Indicate the mood of the syllogism.
    3) Indicate whether the syllogism is valid or invalid and why.
    4) Change each invalid syllogism to a valid one by changing either element of the major premise or the entire minor premise from affirmative to negative or vice-versa.

Example: Socrates cannot be both a farmer and a philosopher
               Socrates is not a farmer
               Therefore, Socrates is a philosopher

    1)   Not both P and Q   2) First invalid mood: *Fallacy of Denying the First Conjunct*.
           Not P
           Therefore Q   3) Invalid (since the syllogism affirms by denying rather than
                                    denying by affirming OR since it is *tollendo ponens* rather than
                                    ponendo tollens)

    4)   Socrates cannot be both a farmer and a philosopher
           Socrates is a farmer
           Therefore, Socrates is not a philosopher

                The syllogism is now of the following form: Not both P and Q
                                                              P
                                                             Therefore, not Q

Bilbo cannot both enjoy the comfort of home and the excitement of adventure
Bilbo enjoys the comfort of home
Therefore, Bilbo does not enjoy the excitement of adventure

Bilbo cannot both enjoy the comfort of home and the excitement of adventure
Bilbo does not enjoy the excitement of adventure
Therefore, Bilbo enjoys the comfort of home

Bilbo cannot both enjoy the comfort of home and the excitement of adventure
Bilbo enjoys the excitement of adventure
Therefore, does not enjoy the comfort of home

Bilbo cannot both enjoy the comfort of home and the excitement of adventure
Bilbo does not enjoy the comfort of home
Therefore, Bilbo enjoys the excitement of adventure

Bilbo cannot both wear the Ring and remain uncorrupted
Bilbo does not remain uncorrupted
Therefore, Bilbo wears the Ring

Bilbo cannot both wear the Ring and remain uncorrupted
Bilbo wears the Ring
Therefore, Bilbo does not remain uncorrupted

Bilbo cannot both wear the Ring and remain uncorrupted
Bilbo remains uncorrupted
Therefore, Bilbo does not wear the Ring

Bilbo cannot both wear the Ring and remain uncorrupted
Bilbo does not wear the Ring
Therefore, Bilbo remains uncorrupted

Read section titled, "Reduction of Conjunctive Syllogisms to Conditional Syllogisms." Read the entire section carefully.

26. Reduce the valid conjunctive syllogisms in question 25 to conditional syllogisms.

_____ **Exercises for Day 3.**

27. Tell whether the following syllogisms are valid or invalid by putting them into proper logical form and indicating the mood. (Notice that some of these arguments are enthymemes, requiring you to determing the missing proposition. Some of these will also need to be converted into logical propositions from ordinary language statements.)

We cannot let developers continue to profit from urban sprawl and expect to preserve what little green space we have left. But no one has put a stop to the developers' rapacious appetites, and consequently we are seeing the slow extinction of rural America.

We cannot both tolerate legalized abortion and claim to be a civilized society, yet we still claim that we are a civilized society.

We cannot complain about the rise in teen pregnancies and yet do nothing about the decline in values that brought the problem about in the first place. Finally, however, we are doing something about this decline.

Religious authority cannot reside in both the church and the Bible. Religious authority does not reside in the church. Therefore, it resides in the Bible.

We cannot both give trade privileges to countries that violate human rights and claim to uphold the cause of freedom and democracy around the world. Yet we claim to be upholding the cause of freedom and democracy around the world. Therefore, we should not give trade privileges to countries that violate human rights.

You cannnot both watch television and not fry your brain. But you watch too much television.

You can't claim to respect the Constitution and then advocate taking guns away from law-abiding citizens. Therefore, you can't claim to respect the Constitution.

You can't say both that public schools are community institutions and then prevent them from reflecting the values and religious beliefs of the community. Yet by saying prayer cannot be allowed in school, you're preventing them from reflecting those values. So why don't you just admit that they aren't community institutions anymore?

Man cannot both be descended from animals and be fundamentally different from animals. But we know that we are fundamentally different from animals. Therefore, we cannot be descended from animals.

We cannot allow the wholesale destruction of our rivers and forests and expect to survive as a species ourselves. Yet we continue to allow the destruction of the environment. We will never survive.

You can have a government-run medical system that's less costly, or a privately-run one that has high-quality care, but you can't have both. Many countries have a government-run system, and quality has suffered.

You can't have a welfare system that hands out checks to people with no strings attached and expect people to still be productive. But our welfare system no longer hands out checks to people with no strings attached. Therefore, people are being productive.

We cannot expect a society where families are falling apart to be a law-abiding society. That's why you see so much crime.

America cannot be both a secular country and a Christian country. Therefore, America is not a secular country.

We cannot be saved both by faith and by works. But we are not saved by works. Therefore, we must be saved by faith.

_____ **Exercises for Day 4.** **Read section titled, "Summary." Read the entire section carefully.**

28. Formulate two of your own examples for each of the two valid moods.

29. Indicate whether the following are true or false:

T	F	There are four valid moods of conjunctive syllogisms.
T	F	All of the invalid moods are *ponendo tollens*.
T	F	A conjunctive syllogism and a disjunctive syllogism are both hypothetical syllogisms.
T	F	The major premise in a conjunctive syllogism is the premise which contains the major term.
T	F	The conjunct is the proposition of a disjunctive statement that appears only in the conclusion.

_____ **Weekly Analysis Assignment.** **Find an article from a newspaper (letters to the editor in newspapers are ideal) or magazine or a chapter from a book you are reading that contains conjunctive reasoning. Either write a short 1-2 page essay or make a presentation in class analyzing the argument. The paper or presentation should contain the following elements:**

1. A *presentation* of the argument as it was originally written.
2. A *summary* of the argument in your own words.
3. An *analysis* of the logical form of the argument.
4. An *evaluation* of the argument's soundness. This will involve assessing both the truth of the argument's premises and its validity. Remember that if the argument is valid and the premises are true, the conclusion must be true. If the argument is valid and one or more of the premises are false, then the conclusion must also be false. And if the argument is invalid, the truth of the conclusion cannot be determined one way or another by knowing the truth of the premises.
5. State your agreement or disagreement with the argument you have analyzed.

The Bible
"You cannot serve both God and Mammon."

_____

_____ **The Argument in Plain Language:** "You can't serve two masters."

_____ **The Argument:** "No servant can serve two masters. Either he will hate the one and love the other, or he will be devoted to the one and despise the other. You cannot serve both God and mammon."
—Jesus, Luke 16:13

_____ **Background of the Argument:** The term "mammon" is sometimes translated "money" but has broader meaning. It means, more generally, wealth for its own sake. Jesus here is pointing out that many people make worldly wealth and possessions into an idol. To do so, he argues, disallows us from claiming to follow God, since idol worship and worship of the true God are incompatible. The form of the argument is very clearly a conjunctive syllogism, but only includes the major premise. The minor premise and the conclusion are determined in each of our lives.

_____ **Assignment:**
1. Formulate the argument in two simple syllogisms, one affirming the first conjunct and another affirming the second conjunct.
2. Write a 1-2 page essay examining which form of the argument applies to the actions of most people today. Do most people serve God or mammon? Is it any different today than it was in Jesus' time? What about your own life?

"Somebody said
that reason was dead...
Reason said, No,
I think not so."

—Anonymous

Polysyllogisms
& Aristotelian Sorites

_____ **Introduction.** Arguments may be either simple or complex. By saying that a thing is simple, we mean that it has relatively few parts. When we say something is complex, we mean that it has relatively more parts. Until now, all the argument forms with which we have dealt have been simple. We now discuss complex arguments (also known as **_chain arguments_**), of which there are four kinds:

- ✓ Polysyllogisms
- ✓ Sorites
- ✓ Epicheirema
- ✓ Dilemmas

In this chapter, we will be discussing the first two of these—polysyllogisms and sorites. We will discuss only the first kind of sorites in this chapter, however, and the second kind we will discuss in the next chapter.

_____ **What is a Polysyllogism?** A **_polysyllogism_** is a syllogism that links together several syllogisms in such a way that the conclusion of one syllogism serves as a premise for the next one.

Here is an example of a polysyllogism:

1) All good students will readily understand polysyllogisms
2) All students of logic are good students
3) Therefore all students of logic will readily understand polysyllogisms
4) But all people who read this book are students of logic
5) Therefore all people who read this book will readily understand polysyllogisms

In this argument, the conclusion (3) of the first argument ((1)-(3)) acts as the major premise for the second argument ((3)-(5)). In this example, both the first argument, and the second (which uses the conclusion of the first as a premise) happen to be BARBARAs.

A _polysyllogism_ **is a syllogism that links together several syllogisms in such a way that the conclusion of one syllogism serves as a premise for the next one.**

This argument has the following structure:

All A is B
All C is A
Therefore, all C is B
All D is C
Therefore, all D is B

Note that the make-up of a polysyllogism need not be limited to two component syllogisms. In fact, it can have any number of component syllogisms.

_____ **Validity of Polysyllogisms.** Dealing with polysyllogisms is not difficult, since they are merely made up of the simpler elements we have already studied; namely, categorical syllogisms. The same rules apply to polysyllogisms that apply to simple syllogisms. The only thing to keep in mind is that the validity of the polysyllogism is dependent upon the validity of all its parts. In other words, in order for a complex polysyllogism to be considered valid, all the simple syllogisms that make it up must be valid. If any one is not, then the whole polysyllogism is to be considered invalid.

The method to follow in determining the validity of a polysyllogism, then, is to test each of the component syllogisms for validity. For example, since the two simple syllogisms that make up our polysyllogism above are both BARBARA, and since we know BARBARA to be a valid form, the polysyllogism itself is therefore valid.

_____ **What is a Sorites?** The second kind of chain argument we will discuss in this chapter is the **sorites** (pronounced "sore eye teez"). The **sorites** is a chain argument which, through a chain of premises (without the intermediate conclusions), connects the subject of the first premise with the predicate of the conclusion.

The word **sorites** comes from the Greek word for **heap**, possibly a reference to the multiple premises included in it. Cicero called it the most deceptive of all arguments, and indeed its complexity makes it especially subject to error.

There are two kinds of sorites: the **Aristotelian** (or **classic**) sorites and the **Goclenian** sorites. We will discuss only the Aristotelian in this chapter. Goclenian sorites will be discussed in the next chapter. The Aristotelian sorites is named, of course, after Aristotle, even though it is not referred to by Aristotle himself.

_____ **The Aristotelian Sorites.** The Aristotelian sorites is a series of Fourth (or Indirect First) Figure syllogisms with all of the conclusions unexpressed except the last. Here is an example:

All students of logic are good students
All good students read this logic book
All people who read this logic book will readily understand sorites
All students who readily understand sorites are intelligent
Therefore, all students of logic are intelligent

In order for a polysyllogism to be considered valid, all the simple syllogisms that make it up must be valid.

This sorites has the following form:

```
All A is B
All B is C
All C is D
All D is E
Therefore, all A is E
```

Notice several things in this argument. First, unlike the polysyllogism, the conclusions in each of the component syllogisms are unexpressed. Although they are not ***explicit***, however, they are ***implicit***: they are lurking there, but we cannot see them without ferreting them out ourselves.

Secondly, notice that in each case, the predicate of the preceding premise is always the subject of the following premise. This provides a series of middle terms (B, C and D) linking each premise to the one after in an unbroken chain of reasoning that ultimately connects together the subject of the first premise with the predicate in the conclusion.

_____ **Extrapolating Aristotelian Sorites.** We call the process of providing the missing conclusions in a sorites ***extrapolation***. Extrapolation of Aristotelian sorites involves converting a series of Fourth Figure syllogisms into a series of First Figure syllogisms. If we do this, we get the following:

All good students read this logic book
All students of logic are good students
      Therefore, all students of logic read this logic book
All people who read this logic book will readily understand sorites
All students of logic read this logic book
      Therefore, all students of logic will readily understand sorites
All students who readily understand sorites are intelligent
All students of logic will readily understand sorites
Therefore, all students of logic are intelligent

All the steps in bold italics are steps we provided in order to fully express the syllogisms in the argument. You can see now that the original sorites was actually made up of three different syllogisms—a fact we can now see because we provided the missing steps.

The extrapolation of an Aristotelian sorites takes the following form:

All B is C
All A is B
Therefore, All A is C
All C is D
All A is C
Therefore, All A is D
All D is E
All A is D
Therefore, All A is E

Extrapolation can be done using the following steps:

1) We switched the first two premises in order to make the first syllogism a First Figure argument. You can see that, whereas the first two premises were originally **prae-sub**, they are now **sub-prae**.

2) We use the conclusion resulting from the first component simple syllogism as the **minor** premise of the next simple syllogism, in order to place the other simple syllogisms in the argument into the First Figure. This is indicated by the arrows.

3) We repeated step 2) until the end of the sorites.

_____ **Validity of Sorites.** Like the polysyllogism, the validity of the sorites depends on the validity of its component parts. If all of the syllogisms that make it up are valid, then the sorites is valid. Here are three simple steps to follow in testing a sorites for validity:

Step #1: Put the sorites in standard form

Step #2: Provide the missing conclusions

Step #3: Test each resulting component syllogism for validity

_____ **Rules for Sorites.** Although the validity of the sorites is dependent upon the validity of its component parts, there are two rules which can be applied to sorites as such:

Rule #1: Only the premise which contains the **minor** term may be particular

Rule #2: Only the premise which contains the **major** term may be negative

Notice that the two rules address particular and negative statements. All of our examples, however, have included only universal affirmative statements. Be aware that sorites can include particular or negative propositions as long as they do not violate these two rules.

_____ **Summary.** Arguments may be simple or complex. There are four kinds of complex arguments:

✓ Polysyllogisms
✓ Sorites
✓ Epicheirema
✓ Dilemmas

In this chapter, we cover polysyllogisms and the first of the two kinds of sorites. A **polysyllogism** is a syllogism that links together several syllogisms in such a way that the conclusion of one syllogism serves as a premise in the next one. The **sorites** is a chain argument which, through a chain of premises (without the intermediate conclusions), connects the subject of the first premise with the predicate of the conclusion.

There are two kinds of sorites: the **Aristotelian** and the **Goclenian**. The Aristotelian sorites is a series of Fourth (or Indirect First) Figure syllogisms with all of the conclusions unexpressed except the last.

Although the validity of the sorites is dependent upon the validity of its component parts, there are two rules which can be applied to sorites as such.

_____ **Exercises for Day 1.** **Peruse entire chapter. Then read the introductory section at the very beginning of chapter 1. Read this section carefully and try to understand it as best you can.**

1. What kind of arguments (simple or complex) are discussed in this chapter?

2. What do we mean when we say that an argument is simple?

3. What do we mean when we say that an argument is complex?

4. List the four kinds of complex arguments.

Read section titled, "What is a Polysyllogism?" Read it carefully.

5. What is a polysyllogism? Explain, in your own words, how a polysyllogism is structured.

6. Show the form of a polysyllogism using the letters U, V, X, Y and Z

7. Complete the polysyllogisms below:

All good students will readily understand polysyllogisms
All students of logic are good students
Therefore _____
But all people who read this book are students of logic
Therefore _____

All animals breathe oxygen
All mammals are animals
Therefore _____
But all bears are mammals
Therefore _____

All men are mortal
All Europeans are men
Therefore _____
But all Romans are Europeans
Therefore _____

All rational animals are human
All Americans are rational animals
Therefore _____
But all Kentuckians are Americans
Therefore _____

8. Create three polysyllogisms (you will want to refer to the form of the polysyllogism shown in the text). Indicate terms in the manner below to help in the construction of the syllogisms. (Choose your component terms so that the arguments make sense.)

A = _____
B = _____
C = _____
D = _____

Read section titled, "Validity of Polysyllogisms." Read it carefully.

9. Explain how the validity of polysyllogisms is determined.

10. Indicate whether the syllogisms you created in Question 8 are valid (they should be if you did them right) and explain why they are valid in accordance with your explanation in question 9.

Exercises for Day 2. Read section titled, "What is a Sorites?" Read it carefully.

11. Explain, in your own words, how a sorites is structured.

12. What are the two kinds of sorites called?

Read section titled, "The Aristotelian Sorites." Read it carefully.

13. What is an Aristotelian sorites?

14. Show the form of the Aristotelian sorites using the letters U, V, X, Y and Z.

15. In what way are sorites similar to polysyllogisms?

16. In what two ways are sorites unlike polysyllogisms?

Read section titled, "Extrapolating Aristotelian Sorites." Read it carefully.

17. Provide the missing steps in the following sorites. (Note that the first two statements have already been switched to yield a First Figure syllogism.)

All men are animals
Peter is a man
    Therefore, _____
All animals are organisms
_____
    Therefore, _____
All organisms have a body
_____
    Therefore, Peter has a body

All polygons are planes
All triangles are polygons
    Therefore, _____
All planes are magnitudes
_____
    Therefore, _____
All magnitudes are quantities
_____
    Therefore, all triangles are quantities

18. Using the three steps discussed in this section of the text, provide the missing steps in the following sorites:

For whom he did foreknow, he also did predestinate ... Moreover whom he did predestinate, them he also called: and whom he called, them he also justified: and whom he justified, them he also glorified.
      -Romans 8:29

All men of revenge have their souls often uneasy; uneasy souls are a plague unto themselves; now, to be one's own plague is folly in the extreme: therefore all men of revenge are extreme fools.
      -Isaac Watts

19. Construct your own Aristotelian sorites.

Read section titled, "Validity of Sorites." Read it carefully.

20. What are the three steps for determining the validity of sorites?

21. Using this three-step method, test the sorites in question 18 for validity.

22. Using the three-step method, test the sorites you constructed in question 19 for validity.

————————— **Exercises for Day 3.** **Read section titled, "Rules for Sorites." Read it carefully.**

23. Put the following Aristotelian sorites in proper form and extrapolate them:

Abortion destroys an innocent human life, and anything that destroys innocent human life is wrong. If something is wrong, then it should be illegal. Therefore, abortion should be illegal.

Television viewing encourages a person to suspend rational thought. Any activity that encourages a person to suspend rational thought will ultimately impair his ability to concentrate. And anything that impairs a person's ability to concentrate should be avoided. Therefore, television viewing should be avoided.

Public schools claim to be community institutions, and any institution that claims to be a community institution should reflect the values of the community. Part of reflecting the values of a community involves allowing people to do the things supported by the community, one example being school prayer. Therefore, public schools should allow school prayer.

Whatever the government gets involved in it messes up. And whatever it messes up ends up costing taxpayers a lot of money. Now the government wants to run the health care industry. So watch your pocketbooks.

————————— **Exercises for Day 4.** **Read section titled, "Summary." Read it carefully.**

24. Indicate whether the following are true or false:

T	F	There are four kinds of complex syllogisms: polysyllogisms, epicheirema, Aristotelian sorites and Goclenian sorites.
T	F	A *polysyllogism* is a syllogism that links together several syllogisms in such a way that the conclusion of one syllogism serves as a premise in the next one.
T	F	The *sorites* is a chain argument which, through a chain of premises (without the intermediate conclusions), connects the predicate of the first premise with the subject of the conclusion.
T	F	There are two kinds of sorites: the *Aristotelian* and the *Galenic*.
T	F	The Aristotelian sorites is a series of Fourth (or Indirect First) Figure syllogisms with all of the conclusions unexpressed except the last.

————————— **Weekly Analysis Assignment.** **Find an article from a newspaper (letters to the editor in newspapers are ideal) or magazine or a chapter from a book you are reading that contains a polysyllogism or a sorites. Either write a short 1-2 page essay or make a presentation in class analyzing the argument. The paper or presentation should contain the following elements:**

1. A *presentation* of the argument as it was originally written.
2. A *summary* of the argument in your own words.
3. An *analysis* of the logical form of the argument.
4. An *evaluation* of the argument's soundness. This will involve assessing both the truth of the argument's premises and its validity. Remember that if the argument is valid and the premises are true, the conclusion must be true. If the argument is valid and one or more of the premises are false, then the conclusion must also be false. And if the argument is invalid, the truth of the conclusion cannot be determined one way or another by knowing the truth of the premises.
5. State your agreement or disagreement with the argument you have analyzed.

Seneca

"The Life of Virtue"

_____

_____ **The Argument in Plain Language:** "The virtuous life is the happy life."

_____ **The Argument:** "Qui prudens est, et temperans est; qui temperans est, et constans est; qui constans est, et imperturbatus est; qui imperturbatus est, sine tristitia est; qui sine tristitia est, beatus est; ergo prudens beatus est, et prudentia ad beatam vitam satis est." Translation: "He who is prudent is temperate; he who is temperate is constant; he who is constant is imperturbable; he who is imperturbable is without sorrow; he who is without sorrow is happy; therefore, he who is prudent is happy, and prudence is sufficient for the happy life."
—**Seneca,** *Epistle 85*

_____ **Background of the Argument:** Seneca (4 B.C.-65 A.D.), who was born in Spain, became for a time the most famous writer and philosopher in all of Rome. Seneca was one of the most famous exponents of the philosophy of Stoicism, a school of philosophy that was founded in the 3rd century B.C. by Zeno of Citium. As a Stoic, Seneca did not believe in a personal God, but that nature as it was was the only reality. He believed that the life of virtue is a life lived in accordance with nature and the rational order of things, and that man must give up worrying about things that he has no power to control and must instead be satisfied with those things which he has the power to change, which consisted primarily of his own ethical behavior. High personal ethical standards characterized practioners of Stoicism. Ironically, Seneca was one of the tutors of Nero, who later became one of Rome's most craven and depraved emperors. No one holds Seneca responsible for this, however, since Nero was well on his way to becoming a monster by the time Seneca came along. And eventually, the opposition of Seneca to Nero's excesses led to his death: forced suicide at the command of the Emperor. Stoicism as it was believed by Seneca came to be the predominant belief of well-educated Romans of the time. Although many of its beliefs were at odds with Christianity, the high standard of virtue espoused by the Stoics was admired by many early Christians, and the ethical principles that characterized many Stoics helped prepare many in the Roman empire for the coming of Christianity. In this argument, an Aristotelian sorites, Seneca argues that happiness is dependent upon the life of virtue.

_____ **Assignment:**
1. Formulate the argument in one complex syllogism.
2. Extrapolate the argument in the manner shown in the text.
3. Indicate whether the argument is sound or unsound. Give reasons for your conclusion.
4. Write a short essay on Seneca or on the beliefs of Stoic philosophy, with special attention to the similarities and differences between these beliefs and Christianity.

"The heart has its reason, which reason cannot know."

—Pascal

Goclenian & Conditional Sorites

_____ **Goclenian Sorites.** In addition to the Aristotelian form of sorites studied in the last chapter, there is a second form, referred to as **Goclenian.** The Goclenian sorites is similar to the Aristotelian, except that the series of syllogisms are First Figure rather than Fourth.

The Aristotelian (or **classic**) sorites is named, of course, after Aristotle. The Goclenian sorites is named after **Goclenius** (1547-1628 A.D.). Goclenius was the first to point out that there was another form of sorites than the Aristotelian form.

Here is an example of a Goclenian sorites:

All students who readily understand sorites are intelligent
All people who read this logic book will readily understand sorites
All good students read this logic book
All students of logic are good students
Therefore, all students of logic are intelligent

Here, the form is somewhat different than the Aristotelian:

All D is E
All C is D
All B is C
All A is B
Therefore, all A is E

Notice first that the premises in this Goclenian sorites are in the exact reverse order of those in the Aristotelian sorites. Second, notice that, instead of the **predicate** of the preceding premise being the **subject** of the following premise, the **subject** of the preceding premise is the **predicate** of the following.

These are indications of something that may not, at first, be obvious; namely, that, while the argument in Aristotelian sorites moves from the less inclusive to the more inclusive, the Goclenian moves from the more inclusive to the less inclusive. Put in logical terms, the Goclenian syllogism moves from the use of middle terms with greater extension to those

Goclenian sorites are similar to the Aristotelian, except that they are First Figure syllogisms rather than Fourth.

with lesser extension, while the Aristotelian moves from middle terms with lesser extension to those with greater extension. The middle terms in a sorites are all the terms in the syllogism with the exception of the minor and major terms (which are the subject and predicate of the conclusion, respectively).

_____ **Extrapolating Goclenian Sorites.** To see the individual syllogisms which make up the more complex sorites, we can look at the following:

> All students who readily understand sorites are intelligent
> All people who read this logic book will readily understand sorites
> > ***Therefore, all people who read this logic book are intelligent***
> All good students read this logic book
> > ***Therefore, all good students are intelligent***
> All students of logic are good students
> Therefore, all students of logic are intelligent

Note that the Goclenian sorites is easier to extrapolate than the Aristotelian, since we need simply to insert the conclusions of the component arguments in their obvious places: there is no need to add any conclusion as a minor premise in any of the later component syllogisms.

The form of the extrapolation of a Goclenian sorites is as follows:

> All D is E
> All C is D
> > ***Therefore, All C is E***
> All B is C
> > ***Therefore, All B is E***
> All A is B
> Therefore, all A is E

We see once again that we have three simple syllogisms which make up the one sorites. Once again we followed some simple steps:

> 1) We used the conclusion of the first two premises as the ***major*** premise of the next simple syllogism
> 2) We repeated step 1)

In Goclenian sorites, instead of making the conclusion of one syllogism the ***minor*** premise of the next, as in Aristotelian sorites, we make it the ***major*** premise of the following syllogism. In Aristotelian sorites we did this somewhat awkward procedure to yield a series of First Figure syllogisms. The order of the premises in Goclenian sorites, however, is naturally first figure, allowing us to leave the conclusion of each component syllogism in its natural place, and using it as the major premise in the next.

The Goclenian sorites is easier to extrapolate than the Aristotelian.

_____ **Distinguishing Sorites.** The differences between Aristotelian and Goclenian sorites can be summarized as follows:

Aristotelian:	**Goclenian:**
Unites the subject of the *first* premise with the predicate of the *last*	Unites the subject of the *last* proposition with the predicate of the *first*
The component simple syllogisms are *Fourth* (Indirect First) Figure	The component simple syllogisms are *First* Figure
Predicate of previous propositions is *subject* of subsequent propositions	*Subject* of previous propositions is *predicate* of subsequent propositions
The first premise is a *minor* premise	The first premise is a *major* premise
Moves from *lesser* extension to *greater* extension	Moves from *greater* extension to *lesser* extension

The contrasting forms of these sorites can be seen this way (with indications of which of them may be particular and which negative):

Aristotelian	**Goclenian**
All (or Some) A is B	All (or No) D is E
All B is C	All C is D
All C is D	All B is C
All (or No) D is E	All (or Some) A is B
Therefore, all (or no or some) A is E	Therefore, all (or some or no) A is E

_____ **Validity of Goclenian Sorites.** The conditions for the validity of the Goclenian sorites is the same as for its Aristotelian cousin: it depends on the validity of its component parts. If all of the syllogisms that make it up are valid, then the sorites is valid. Here are three simple steps to follow in testing a sorites for validity:

Step #1: Unless it already is, put the sorites in standard form (i.e. in one of the two forms just above for Aristotelian or Goclenian)

Step #2: Provide the missing conclusions

Step #3: Test each resulting component syllogism for validity

_____ **Rules for Goclenian Sorites.** In addition, the same two rules apply to Goclenian Sorites as to the Aristotelian:

Rule #1: Only the premise which contains the *minor* term may be particular

Rule #2: Only the premise which contains the *major* term may be negative

Remember that sorites can include particular or negative propositions as long as they do not violate these two rules. (See the above comparison to determine the possible quantity and quality of statements in sorites.)

The conditions for the validity of the Goclenian sorites are the same as for its Aristotelian cousin.

The conditional sorites is simply a sorites made up of a series of conditional statements, each of which (except the first) has, as its antecedent, the consequent of the previous premise.

_____ **Conditional Sorites.** There is one additional form of sorites that we should consider, and that is conditional sorites. A conditional sorites is simply a sorites made up of a series of conditional statements, each of which (except the first) has as its antecedent the consequent of the preceding premise. Conditional sorites can take one of four valid forms:

Pure Conditional Sorites

If A, then B	If A, then B
If B, then C	If B, then C
If C, then D	If C, then D
<u>If D, then E</u>	<u>If D, then E</u>
Therefore, if A, then E	Therefore, if not E, then not A

Mixed Conditional Sorites

If A, then B	If A, then B
If B, then C	If B, then C
If C, then D	If C, then D
If D, then E	If D, then E
<u>But A</u>	<u>But not E</u>
Therefore, E	Therefore, not A

_____ **Validity of Conditional Sorites.** Notice that the rules governing conditional sorites are similar to those that govern standard conditional syllogisms:

They must affirm the antecedent of the first premise

OR

They must deny the consequent in the last conditional premise

As you can see, the pure conditional sorites are just a more complex form of a pure conditional syllogism (since all the premises are conditional statements). They affirm the first antecedent or deny the last consequent in the antecedent of the conclusion itself. The mixed conditional sorites are similar to mixed conditionals in that they include as one of their premises (the last one) a categorical statement. In these, the appropriate affirmation or denial is performed in a separate, final premise.

_____ **Summary.** There are two kinds of sorites: the **_Aristotelian_** and the **_Goclenian_**. In this chapter, we cover Goclenian sorites. Goclenian sorites are similar to the Aristotelian, except that the series of syllogisms are **_First Figure_** rather than **_Fourth_**.

The validity of Goclenian sorites is the same as that which applies to the Aristotelian: it depends on **_the validity of the component syllogisms_** of which it is comprised. The same two rules apply also to both Goclenian and Aristotelian sorites.

There are also conditional sorites, of which there are four valid forms.

Sorites

The Two Forms of Categorical Sorites:

<u>Aristotelian</u>	<u>Goclenian</u>
All (or Some) A is B	All (or No) D is E
All B is C	All C is D
All C is D	All B is C
All (or No) D is E	All (or Some) A is B
Therefore, all (or no or some) A is E	Therefore, all (or some or no) A is E

The Characteristics of the two forms of Categorical Sorites:

Unites the subject of the **first** premise with the predicate of the **last**	Unites the subject of the **last** proposition with the predicate of the **first**
The component simple syllogisms are **Fourth** (Indirect First) Figure	The component simple syllogisms are **First** Figure
Predicate of previous propositions is **subject** of subsequent propositions	**Subject** of previous propositions is **predicate** of subsequent propositions
The first premise is a **minor** premise	The first premise is a **major** premise
Moves from **lesser** extension to **greater** extension	Moves from **greater** extension to **lesser** extension

The Four Valid Forms of Conditional Sorites:

<u>Pure Conditional Sorites</u>

If A, then B	If A, then B
If B, then C	If B, then C
If C, then D	If C, then D
<u>If D, then E</u>	<u>If D, then E</u>
Therefore, if A, then E	Therefore, if not E, then not A

<u>Mixed Conditional Sorites</u>

If A, then B	If A, then B
If B, then C	If B, then C
If C, then D	If C, then D
If D, then E	If D, then E
<u>But A</u>	<u>But not E</u>
Therefore, E	Therefore, not A

_____ **Exercises for Day I.** **Peruse entire chapter. Read section titled, "Goclenian Sorites." Read it carefully.**

1. Show the form of the Goclenian sorites using the letters A, B, C, D and E.

Read section titled, "Extrapolating Goclenian Sorites." Read it carefully.

2. Provide the missing steps in the following sorites:

All organisms have a body
All animals are organisms
    Therefore, _____
All men are animals
    Therefore, _____
Peter is a man
Therefore, Peter has a body

All magnitudes are quantities
All planes are magnitudes
    Therefore, _____
All polygons are planes
    Therefore, _____
All triangles are polygons
Therefore, all triangles are quantities

3. Construct your own Goclenian sorites.

Read section titled, "Distinguishing Sorites." Read it carefully.

4. State five characteristics which differentiate Aristotelian from Goclenian sorites.

5. Indicate whether the pattern of reasoning in the following sorites is Aristotelian or Goclenian:

The longer life the more offence,
The more offence the greater paine,
The greater paine the lesse defence,
The less defence the lesser gaine;
The loos of gaine long yll doth trye,
Wherefore come death and let mee dye.

Come gentle Death, the ebbe of care,
The ebbe of care the flood of life,
The flood of life the joyfull fare,
The joyfull fare the end of strife,
The end of strife that thing wish I;
Where come death and let mee dye.

—Sir Thomas Wyatt

Read section titled, "Validity of Goclenian Sorites." Read it carefully.

6. What are the three steps for determining the validity of sorites?

7. Using the three-step method, test the sorites you constructed in question 3 for validity. If it is invalid, put it into a valid form.

Read section titled, "Rules for Goclenian Sorites." Read it carefully.

8. List the three rules that apply to sorites.

9. Apply the two rules for sorites to the sorites you constructed in question 3.

         Traditional Logic

_____ **Exercises for Day 2.**

10. Extrapolate the following sorites:

Any society that experiences a breakdown of moral values is a society whose children will suffer. A society that is seeing high rates of illegitimacy, welfare dependency and crime is a society which is obviously experiencing moral breakdown. America is experiencing high rates of illegitimacy, welfare dependency and crime. Therefore, America's children will suffer.

We should only give special trade privileges to those countries who respect human rights. Any country that imprisons its people for political reasons has no respect for human rights. We know that China imprisons people for political reasons. Therefore, we should not give special trade privileges to China.

We should pass no law that conflicts with the Constitution. Any law that violates a section of the Bill of Rights conflicts with the Constitution. Laws that restrict gun ownership are laws that violate a section of the Bill of Rights. Therefore, we should not pass laws that restrict gun ownership.

The stifling of individual productivity will eventually strangle the American economy. The growth of government stifles individual productivity. If we pass more social spending programs, there will be more growth in government. If we elect more liberals to congress, there will be more social spending programs. Therefore, the election of more liberals to congress will eventually strangle the American economy.

_____ **Exercises for Day 3.** **Read section titled, "Conditional Sorites." Read it carefully.**

11. Write out the forms of the four valid forms of conditional sorites, using the letters A - E.

12. Identify which of the four forms of conditional sorites each of the following exemplifies. (Note that some of these are also enthymemes.)

If evolution is true, then we are nothing more than the products of chance, and if we are products of chance, then our thoughts are the product of chance. And if our thoughts are the product of chance, then there is no such thing as right and wrong (since it is the product of a physically determined process rather than reflective of some real standard we all recognize). And if there is no such thing as right and wrong, then we ought to be allowed to do anything we want, even if it harms other people. But we cannot do things that harm other people. Therefore, evolution is false.

If poverty causes crime, then there should be more crime in times of poverty and less in times of prosperity. And if there is more crime in times of poverty and less in times of prosperity, then we should we should focus our anti-crime efforts on reducing poverty. If we focus our efforts in this way, then we should see a decline in both poverty and crime. But we have not seen a decline in either.

If welfare programs continue, we will continue to reward sloth. And if we encourage sloth, the people of our country will lose their work ethic. If people in our country lose their work ethic, then our standard of living will go down. Therefore, if welfare programs continue, our standard of living will go down.

If public schools succeed in teaching children basic academic skills, then they will learn how to read and write. And if children learn how to read a write, they will grow up literate. If children in this country grow up literate, they will be able to share in the American dream. Therefore, if children are to share in the American dream, then public schools must succeed in teaching children basic academic skills.

13. Construct your own conditional sorites in each of the four valid forms.

_____ **Exercises for Day 4.** **Read section titled, "Summary." Read it carefully.**

14. Indicate whether the following are true or false:

T F   There are two kinds of sorites: affirmative and negative.

T F   Goclenian sorites are similar to the Aristotelian, except that the series of syllogisms are *First Figure*
            rather than *Fourth*.

T F   The validity of Goclenian sorites depends on the validity of the component syllogisms of which it is comprised.

T F   There are five valid forms of conditional sorites.

_____ **Weekly Analysis Assignment.** **Find an article from a newspaper (letters to the
editor in newspapers are ideal) or magazine or a chapter from a book you are reading that contains a
polysyllogism or a sorites. Either write a short 1-2 page essay or make a presentation in class analyzing
the argument. The paper or presentation should contain the following elements:**

1. A *presentation* of the argument as it was originally written.
2. A *summary* of the argument in your own words.
3. An *analysis* of the logical form of the argument.
4. An *evaluation* of the argument's soundness. This will involve assessing both the truth of the argument's premises and its
validity. Remember that if the argument is valid and the premises are true, the conclusion must be true. If the argument is valid
and one or more of the premises are false, then the conclusion must also be false. And if the argument is invalid, the truth of the
conclusion cannot be determined one way or another by knowing the truth of the premises.
5. State your agreement or disagreement with the argument you have analyzed.

William Shakespeare

"Thou art in a parlous state, Shepherd"

_____The Argument:

Touchstone: Wast ever in court, Shepherd?
Corin: No, truly.
Touchstone: Then thou art damned.
Corin: Nay, I hope not.
Touchstone: Truly, thou art damned, like an ill-roasted egg on one side.
Corin: For not being at court? Your reason.
Touchstone: Why, if thou never wast at court, thou never sawest good manners; if thou never sawest good manners, then thy manners must be wicked, and wickedness is sin, and sin is damnation. Thou art in a parlous state, Shepherd.

—**William Shakespeare,** *As You Like It*, **Act III, Scene II**

_____ **Background of the Argument:** This is an excerpt from a conversation between Touchstone, the court clown, and Corin, a shepherd. Touchstone argues that the refined manners of the royal court are not just convenient social conventions, but absolute moral requirements. By placing these words into the mouth of a fool, Shakespeare seems to be lampooning the idea that the particular manners of a certain time and place are also universal moral imperatives. The shepherd maintains that manners (unlike moral standards) are relative conventions that differ in different social circumstances. This is just one of many examples of the use of logical argument forms used in literature. Corin responds to Touchstone as follows: "Not a whit, Touchstone: those that are good manners at the court are as ridiculous in the country as the behavior of the country is most mockable at the court. You told me you salute not at the court, but that you kiss your hands: that courtesy would be uncleanly, if courtiers were shepherds." Here, the shepherd points out that, if people in the country followed the manners at court, where kissing the hand of another is a form of greeting, they would be creating a health hazard, since the hands of shepherds and others who live in the country are often soiled. In taking Touchstone's logic to its absurd conclusion—that shepherds should act with the same forms of courtesy as courtiers, Corin is performing what is called *reductio ad absurdum*. This is a Latin phrase which means "reduction to absurdity."

_____Assignment:

1. Put the argument into the standard form of a sorites. Determine whether it is an Aristotelian or Goclenian sorites.
2. Put Corin's response in the form of a syllogism.
3. Write a short 1-2 page essay on whether you agree with Touchstone—who believes that manners are universal, like morality—or with Corin—who believes that manners are relative to time and circumstance. Read Act III, Scene II of *As You Like It* and, depending on your position, say what is wrong with Touchstone or Corin's argument.

"Whom God wishes to destroy, he first deprives of reason."

—John Dryden

Epicheirema

_____ **What are epicheirema?** Another kind of chain argument, similar to the sorites, is the ***epicheireme***. Ephicheirema (the plural of epicheireme) are syllogisms in which ***at least one*** of the premises contains causal propositions. A causal proposition is a proposition which includes the proof for the proposition or the reason for believing the proposition to be true.

The causal proposition is usually introduced by the words ***for***, ***since*** or ***because***.

An example of an epicheireme is as follows:

All martyrs are saints ***because all martyrs possess heroic charity***
Peter is a martyr
Therefore, Peter is a saint

In this case, the causal proposition (seen in bold italics) is included in the major premise. This epicheireme is, in fact, one of three possible kinds of epicheirema in accordance with which premise (or premises) contains the causal proposition.

_____ **First Order Epicheirema.** First Order epicheirema are those in which the causal proposition is ***in the major premise***. This form of epicheirema, once its entire logical structure is made explicit, resembles the Goclenian sorites. The epicheireme above is of the First Order.

First Order epicheirema take the following form:

All M is P, ***since r***
All S is a M
Therefore, S is a P

where ***r*** is the ***reason*** or ***proof*** of the proposition that precedes it.

Epicheirema
are syllogisms
in which *at
least one* of the
premises
contain causal
propositions.

_____ **Second Order Epicheirema.** Second Order epicheirema are those in which the causal proposition is *in the minor premise*. This form of epicheirema, once its logical structure is explicit, resembles the Aristotelian sorites. The following syllogism is an example of a Second Order epicheireme:

> All martyrs are saints
> Peter is a martyr *because Peter died for the Faith*
> Therefore, Peter is a saint

Second Order epicheirema take the following form:

> All M is P
> All S is a M, *since r*
> Therefore, S is P

_____ **Third Order Epicheirema.** Third Order epicheirema are compounds of First and Second Order epicheirema in which there are causal propositions in *both the major and the minor premises*. The following syllogism is an example of a Third Order epicheireme:

> All martyrs are saints *since all martyrs possess heroic charity*
> Peter is a martyr, *since Peter died for the Faith*
> Therefore, Peter is a saint

Third Order epicheirema take the following form:

> All M is P, *since r₁*
> All S is a M, *since r₂*
> Therefore, S is P

_____ **Extrapolating Epicheirema of the First Order.** As with sorites, we must make certain propositions within Epicheirema explicit in order to determine their validity. We do this in a way similar to the way in which we treated sorites.

Let's take our First Order epicheireme:

> All martyrs are saints *because all martyrs possess heroic charity*
> Peter is a martyr
> Therefore, Peter is a saint

What we must take into account is that the first premise is itself an abbreviated syllogism, the first part of which (***All martyrs are saints***) is its conclusion. It is then used in the epicheireme as the major premise.

Our job, then is to draw out the full syllogism implicit in the major premise. This first premise gives us the three terms we must use in this process: ***martyrs***, ***saints***, and ***people who possess heroic charity***. But how do we arrange them in the syllogism?

Knowing what we do from previous chapters, this is easy. We know that the first proposition in the major premise (the part not in italics) is to be the conclusion of this new syllogism. Therefore, we know what the minor and major terms of this new syllogism are: ***martyrs*** is the minor

As with sorites, we must make certain propositions within epicheirema explicit in order to determine their validity.

term and **saints** is the major term. That leaves **people who possess heroic charity** as our middle term. We know that the major premise will be in the first premise and the minor in the second. But where in each premise? The subject or predicate?

In order to keep the syllogism as straightforward as possible, we will make it a First Figure (BARBARA in this case, since all the statements are A statements). Since it will be a First Figure, we know where the middle term should appear in each premise. First Figure is *sub-prae*—in other words, the middle term will appear in the subject of the first (or major) premise and the predicate of the second (or minor) premise. Now we know what we must do, and we get the following:

All martyrs are saints
    Proof: *All people who possess heroic charity are saints*
            All martyrs are people who possess heroic charity
            Therefore, all marytrs are saints
Peter is a martyr
Therefore, Peter is a saint

Notice that, using the reasoning we just explained, we turned the causal proposition that was a part of the original major premise into two new, separate premises, justifying the conclusion (which was just the original major premise).

_____ **Extrapolating Epicheirema of the Second Order.** Second Order epicheirema—in which the minor premise contains the causal proposition—must be treated in a manner similar to Aristotelian sorites. Let's take another look at our Second Order epicheireme:

All martyrs are saints
Peter is a martyr **because Peter died for the Faith**
Therefore, Peter is a saint

Here it is the minor premise which contains the causal proposition. We know that the minor premise will be the conclusion of another syllogism, which gives the reason or proof for the minor premise. We take the causal proposition from the minor premise and use it as a basis of another simple syllogism, embedded in the original one.

Once again we know that the major term will be **martyrs**, the minor term **Peter,** and the middle term **people who die for the Faith.** Placing them in their proper arrangement, we get the following:

All martyrs are saints
Peter is a martyr
    Proof: *All people who die for the Faith are martyrs*
            Peter is a person who died for his faith
            Therefore, Peter is a martyr
Therefore, Peter is a saint

You should see the similarity here with the Aristotelian sorites in that it is the minor premise which is the basis for making the reasoning more explicit.

Second order epicheirema must be treated in a manner similar to Aristotelian sorites.

In the Third Order, we combine the processes used in the First and Second Orders.

———————— **Extrapolating Epicheirema of the Third Order.** In the Third Order, we combine the processes we used in the First and Second Order. This will require us to end up with three syllogisms in all, rather than two, since there will be two causal statements (one in the major and one in the minor premise) which must be made explicit.

Our Third Order epicheireme looked like this:

All martyrs are saints *since all martyrs possess heroic charity*
Peter is a martyr, *since Peter died for the Faith*
Therefore, Peter is a saint

We will simply apply the procedure of the First Order in making the major premise explicit and the procedure of the Second Order in making the minor premise explicit. We would end up, therefore, with the following:

All martyrs are saints
    Proof: *All people who possess heroic charity are saints*
               All martyrs are people who possess heroic charity
               Therefore, all marytrs are saints
Peter is a martyr
    Proof: *All people who die for the Faith are martyrs*
               Peter is a person who died for his faith
               Therefore, Peter is a martyr
Therefore, Peter is a saint

Now we have the compound syllogism in a form that allows us to test for its validity. Once again, as with any other compound syllogism, its validity depends upon the validity of all its component syllogisms.

———————— **Summary.** Ephicheirema are syllogisms in which **at least one** of the premises contain causal propositions. A causal proposition is a proposition which includes the proof for the proposition or the reason for believing the proposition to be true.

First Order epicheirema are those in which the causal proposition is **in the major premise**. Second Order epicheirema are those in which the causal proposition is **in the minor premise**. Third Order epicheirema are compounds of First and Second Order epicheirema in which there are causal propositions in **both the major and the minor premises**.

We must make explicit certain propositions within Epicheirema in order to determine their validity. We call this **extrapolation**. We do this in a way similar to the way in which we treated sorites.

There is a structural similarity between First Order epicheirema and Goclenian sorites, as well as a similarity between Second Order epicheirema and Aristotelian sorites. Like Goclenian sorites, it is the **major premise** in First Order epicheirema that must be extrapolated. Like Aristotelian sorites, it is the **minor premise** in Second Order epicheirama that must be extrapolated.

Third Order epicheirema are extrapolated by simply employing both the methods used in the First and Second Orders in combination.

_____ **Exercises for Day I.** **Peruse entire chapter. Then read section titled, "What are Epicheirema?"** **Read this section carefully and try to understand it as best you can.**

1. What are epicheirema?

2. What is a causal proposition?

3. What kind of syllogism is an epicheireme (simple or complex)?

4. List the four kinds of complex (or compound) arguments. [Review]

Read section titled, "First Order Epicheirema." Read it carefully.

5. What is a First Order epicheireme?

6. To what kind of sorites are First Order epicheirema similar?

7. Explain in your own words how a First Order epicheireme is constructed.

8. Construct your own First Order epicheireme.

Read section titled, "Second Order Epicheirema." Read it carefully.

9. What is a Second Order epicheireme?

10. To what kind of sorites is it similar?

11. Explain in your own words how a Second Order epicheireme is constructed.

12. Construct your own Second Order epicheireme.

Read section titled, "Third Order Epicheirema." Read it carefully.

13. What is a Third Order epicheireme?

14. Explain in your own words how a Third Order epicheireme is constructed.

15. Construct your own Third Order epicheireme.

_____ **Exercises for Day 2.** **Read section titled, "Extrapolating Epicheirema of the First Order." Read it carefully.**

16. Take the following epicheirema and extrapolate them, filling in the blank lines with the implicit syllogism contained in the causal statement.

Original epicheireme:
All men are mortal because all men are organisms
Socrates is a man
Therefore, Socrates is mortal

Extrapolated epicheireme:
All men are mortal
   Proof: _____

      _____
      Therefore, all men are mortal
Socrates is a man
Therefore, Socrates is mortal

Original epicheireme:
All cats are exasperating, since they are independent
No exasperating thing is worth having
Therefore, no cat is worth having

Extrapolated epicheireme:
All cats are exasperating
   Proof: _____

      _____
      Therefore, all cats are exasperating
No exasperating thing is worth having
Therefore, no cat is worth having

17. Take the epicheireme you constructed in question 8 and extrapolate it.

Read section titled, "Extrapolating Epicheirema of the Second Order." Read it carefully.

18. Take the following epicheirema and extrapolate them, filling in the blank lines with the implicit syllogism contained in the causal statement.

Original epicheireme:
All men are mortal
Socrates is a man because Socrates is rational
Therefore, Socrates is a mortal

Extrapolated epicheireme:
All men are mortal
Socrates is a man
   Proof: _____

      _____
      Therefore, Socrates is a man
Therefore, Socrates is mortal

Original epicheireme:
All cats are exasperating
No exasperating thing is worth having, since they only bring trouble
Therefore, no cat is worth having

Extrapolated epicheireme:
All cats are exasperating
No exasperating thing is worth having
   Proof: _____

      _____
      Therefore, no exasperating thing is worth having
Therefore, all cats are not worth having

19. Take the epicheireme you constructed in question 12. and extrapolate it.

_____ **Exercises for Day 3.** **Read section titled, "Extrapolating Epicheirema of the Third Order." Read it carefully.**

20. Take the following epicheirema and extrapolate them, filling in the blank lines with the implicit syllogism contained in the causal statement:

Original epicheireme:
All men are mortal because they are not gods
Socrates is a man, since Socrates is a rational animal
Therefore, Socrates is mortal

Extrapolated epicheireme:
All men are mortal
   Proof: _____

      _____
      Therefore, all men are mortal
Socrates is a man
   Proof: _____

      _____
      Therefore, Socrates is a man
Therefore, Socrates is mortal

Original epicheireme:

All cats are exasperating, since they are independent

No exasperating thing is worth having, since they only bring trouble

Therefore, no cat is worth having

Extrapolated epicheireme:

All cats are exasperating

> *Proof:* _____
>
> _____
>
> *Therefore, all cats are exasperating*

No exasperating thing is worth having

> *Proof:* _____
>
> _____
>
> *Therefore, no exasperating thing is worth having*

Therefore, no cat is worth having

21. Take the epicheireme you constructed in question 15 and extrapolate.

22. Using the three steps discussed in this section of the text, provide the missing steps in the following epicheirema:

> "Every rational creature is free by the very fact that he is endowed with intelligence, but man is a rational creature, therefore he is free."
>
> **-Jacques Maritain**

> "Sickness may be good for us; for it weans us from the pleasures of life, and makes us think of dying. But we are uneasy under sickness, which appears by our impatience, complaints, groaning, etc. Therefore, we are uneasy sometimes under that which is good for us."
>
> **-Isaac Watts**

23. Determine the validity of the epicheireme you constructed in question 8.

24. Determine the validity of the epicheireme you constructed in question 12.

25. Determine the validity of the epicheireme you constructed in question 15.

26. Extrapolate the following epicheirema. (Notice that some of these epicheirema are also enthymemes. If they are, provide the missing premise) and indicate whether each is valid. If it is valid and in a figure other than the First, reduce to a First Figure syllogism:

> Abortion destroys an innocent human life, since a fetus is an innocent human life. Any action that destroys innocent human life is wrong. Therefore, abortion is wrong.

> If the Constitution protects the right to keep and bear arms, then gun control laws should be rejected, since no law can violate the Constitution. And we know that the Constitution protects the right to keep and bear arms. Therefore, gun control laws should be rejected.

> If we do not pass fair trade laws, then small companies will go out of business, since they cannot purchase their merchandise as cheaply as larger companies. And if small companies go out of business, our economy will suffer, since small business makes up a large portion of our prosperity.

> Nothing that possesses characteristics that could not be the product of evolution can be the product of evolution. Humans possess intellectual characteristics that could not be the product of evolution, since men possess a rational soul. Therefore, humans cannot be the product of evolution.

> Whenever the government gets involved in something, it creates more problems than it solves, because government is so inefficient. Now the government wants to run the health care system!

The destruction of the environment will ultimately be the undoing of the human race, since we cannot live on an unlivable planet. Therefore, polluters need to pay a heavier price for violating clean air and water standards.

Everyone knows that if you reward sloth, you get more of it, since when you subsidize something, you get more of it. The welfare system rewards sloth, since it gives money to people for not working. Therefore, the welfare system will produce more sloth.

No society that loses its religious foundations can prosper for very long, since moral decline always follows from the loss of religious belief. America is fast turning into such a society, since schools and families have forgotten the importance of passing on their religious heritage to their children.

_____ **Exercises for Day 4.** **Read section titled, "Summary." Read it carefully.**

27. Indicate whether the following are true or false:

T	F	Epicheirema are syllogisms in which at least one of the premises contains a causal proposition.
T	F	A causal proposition is a proposition which is the proof for another proposition or the reason for believing the other proposition to be false.
T	F	First Order epicheirema are epicheirema in which the causal proposition is in the minor premise.
T	F	Third Order epicheirema are similar to Aristotelian sorites.
T	F	In order to check the validity of epicheirema, we must first extrapolate them.
T	F	Like Aristotelian sorites, it is the minor premise in Second Order epicheirema that must be extrapolated.

_____ **Weekly Analysis Assignment. Find an article from a newspaper (letters to the editor in newspapers are ideal) or magazine or a chapter from a book you are reading that contains one or more epicheirema. Either write a short 1-2 page essay or make a presentation in class analyzing the argument. The paper or presentation should contain the following elements:**

1. A *presentation* of the argument as it was originally written.
2. A *summary* of the argument in your own words.
3. An *analysis* of the logical form of the argument, including an extrapolation of whatever epicheireme you are dealing with.
4. An *evaluation* of the argument's soundness. This will involve assessing both the truth of the argument's premises and its validity. Remember that if the argument is valid and the premises are true, the conclusion must be true. If the argument is valid and one or more of the premises are false, then the conclusion must also be false. And if the argument is invalid, the truth of the conclusion cannot be determined one way or another by knowing the truth of the premises.
5. State your agreement or disagreement with the argument you have analyzed.

St. Thomas Aquinas

The Cosmological Argument for the Existence of God

_____ **The Argument in Plain Language:** "There just has to be a reason for things."

_____ **The Argument:** "We find in nature things that are possible to be and not to be, since they are found to be generated, and to corrupt, and consequently, they are possible to be and not to be. But it is impossible for these always to exist, for that which is possible not to be at some time is not. Therefore, if everything is possible not to be, then at one time there could have been nothing in existence. Now if this were true, even now there would be nothing in existence, because that which does not exist only begins to exist by something already existing. Therefore, if at one time nothing was in existence, it would have been impossible for anything to have begun to exist; and thus even now nothing would be in existence—which is absurd. Therefore, not all beings are merely possible, but there must exist something the existence of which is necessary. But every necessary thing either has its necessity caused by another, or not. Now it is impossible to go on to infinity in necessary things which have their necessity caused by another, as has been already proved in regard to efficient causes. Therefore we cannot but postulate the existence of some being having of itself its own necessity, and not receiving it from another, but rather causing in others their necessity. This all men speak of as God."

    —St. Thomas Aquinas, *Summa Theologica*, First Part, Question 2

_____ **Background of the Argument:** The cosmological argument (sometimes known as the "argument from contingency," was first used by Aristotle in the 4th century B. C., but the most famous statement of the argument was by St. Thomas Aquinas. St. Thomas, who was known as the "universal doctor," was a monk who lived in the 13th century. Thomas said that there were five ways to prove God's existence. The form of the cosmological argument discussed here is the third of these. It is from the *Summa Theologica*, one of the greatest single works every produced by an individual thinker. One of the strengths of the argument is that it begins with the everyday world as we know it, and appeals to the sense in all of us that everything must have a cause.

_____ **Assignment:**
    1. Find three epicheirema in this argument.
    2. Write out the argument, as best you can, with all the component syllogisms expressed in proper logical form.
    3. Write a 3-4 page biographical essay on St. Thomas Aquinas.

"Histories make men wise; poets, witty; the mathematics, subtile; natural philosophy, deep; moral, grave; logic and rhetoric, able to contend."

—Francis Bacon

The Dilemma

_____ **What is a Dilemma?** Our fourth and last type of compound syllogism is the ***dilemma***. Of the four kinds of compound syllogisms, dilemmas are perhaps the most interesting. According to Ferdinand Schiller, the dilemma "is the prettiest and dialectically the most effective form of conditional reasoning."

A dilemma is a ***two-horned*** or ***two-edged*** argument which presents, as the major premise, a complex conjunctive proposition in which each of the conjuncts (the ***horns***) is a conditional statement, as well as a minor premise, a disjunctive proposition, in which either the antecedents of the major premise are confirmed, or its consequents are denied.

The dilemma takes four forms. There are three rules with which dilemmas must comply. And there are three strategies that may be employed in answering them.

_____ **The Classification of Dilemmas.** ***Quantitatively***, arguments can be divided into the ***simple*** and the ***complex***. ***Qualitatively***, they can be divided into the ***constructive*** and the ***destructive***. Taking both quantity and quality into account, therefore, there are four different forms of the dilemma:

- ✓ The simple constructive dilemma
- ✓ The simple destructive dilemma
- ✓ The complex constructive dilemma
- ✓ The complex destructive dilemma

_____ **The Simple Constructive Dilemma.** A ***simple constructive*** dilemma is a dilemma in which both of the antecedents of the major premise are affirmed by the minor premise, but in which the consequents in both conjuncts of the major premise are the same.

Here is an example of a simple constructive dilemma that is taken from the ancient case of Protagoras, the great Greek sophist, and Euthlus, his pupil. Protagoras had agreed to teach Euthlus on the following condition: that Euthlus agree to pay Protagorus half his fee

The dilemma is "the prettiest and dialectically the most effective form of conditional reasoning."

— Ferdinand Schiller

when his studies were completed and the other half when Euthlus had won his first case in court. Euthlus paid Protagoras half his fee when the course was completed. But some time went by and Euthlus had still not paid Protagoras the other half of his fee because Euthlus had not yet tried a case in court. Protagoras, worried that he would never be paid the other half, brought suit against Euthlus, forcing him to try his first case.

Protagoras, therefore, argued as follows:

> Euthlus must either win the case or lose it
> If Euthlus loses his case, then he should pay me (because the court will have decided against him); and If Euthlus wins the case, then he should pay me (in accordance with our original agreement)
> Therefore, in either case, he should pay me

Notice that, here, the minor premise is stated first. In constructive dilemmas, this is often done to avoid sounding awkward. But we will note its form by placing the major premise at the beginning:

> If P, then Q; and if R, then Q
> Either P or R
> Therefore, Q

There are three rules with which dilemmas must comply. And there are three strategies that may be used in answering them.

Notice that, although there are two antecedents in the major premise, there is only one consequent: Q. Notice also that each disjunct in the second premise affirms the antecedent of each of the conditional statements in the first premise, yielding the consequent of both of these conditional statements: Q.

_____ **The Simple Destructive Dilemma.** A *simple destructive* dilemma is a dilemma in which both of the consequents of the major premise are denied in the minor premise, but in which the antecedents in both conjuncts of the major premise are the same. Here is an example:

> If I am to be happy, then I must please both God and men
> But either I must displease God (by pleasing man), or I must displease men (by pleasing God)
> Therefore, I cannot be happy

In this case the structure is somewhat different:

> If P, then Q; and if P, then R
> Either *not* Q or *not* R
> Therefore, *not* P

In this case, although there are two consequents in the major premise, there is only one antecedent. In the minor premise, the two consequents are alternatively denied, thereby denying the common antecedent: P.

_____ **The Complex Constructive Dilemma.** A *complex constructive dilemma* is a dilemma in which both of the antecedents of the major premise are affirmed by the minor premise, but in which the consequents in both conjuncts of the major premise are different. Here is an example of a complex constructive dilemma:

> Either Jesus will urge that the woman caught in adultery be stoned or he will urge that she be pardoned
> But if Jesus urges that the woman caught in adultery be stoned, he will be unpopular with the people because of his severity; and if he urges that she be pardoned, then he will be criticized by the Pharisees for disregarding the law of Moses
> Therefore, either Jesus will be unpopular with the people for his severity or he will be criticized by the Pharisees for disregarding the law of Moses

Once again, since this is a constructive dilemma, we see the minor premise stated first. In symbolic notation, the complex constructive dilemma looks like this:

> If P, then Q; and if R, then S
> Either P or R
> Therefore, either Q or S

Notice that there are two antecedents and two consequents in the major premise. Notice also that each disjunct in the second premise affirms the antecedent of each of the conditional statements in the first premise, yielding the consequent of both of these conditional statements, which includes both consequents from the major premise: Q and S.

_____ **The Complex Destructive Dilemma.** A *complex destructive* dilemma is a dilemma in which both of the consequents of the major premise are denied in the minor premise, yielding the negation of the antecedent in both conjuncts of the major premise (which are different) in the conclusion. Here is an example:

> If a man is wise, he will not speak irreverently of holy things in jest
> If a man is good, he will not do it in earnest
> But he must either speak in jest or in earnest
> Therefore, he is either not wise or not good

The form of the complex destructive dilemma is as follows:

> If P, then Q and if R, then S
> Either *not* Q or *not* S
> Therefore, *not* P or *not* R

_____ **Rules for the Dilemma.** There are three rules that must be followed in order for a dilemma to be considered to be properly constructed, each pertaining to a distinct part of the syllogism:

> **Rule #1** (concerning the *major premise*): The consequents in the major premise must follow legitimately from the antecedents (in other words, the major premise must be true)
> **Rule #2** (concerning the *minor premise*): The disjunction in the minor premise must be complete (in other words, there must be no third possibility)

There are three rules which must be followed in order for a dilemma to be considered properly constructed.

> **Rule #3** (concerning the **conclusion**): The conclusion must be exclusive (in other words, it should be the only one that can be inferred from the premises)

The rule violated (if any) will determine the approach an opponent can take to refute the dilemma.

_____ Grasping the Dilemma by the Horns. The dilemma is sometimes referred to as *syllogismus cornitus*, literally, **_horned argument_**. The **_horns_** of a dilemma are the two conditional statements in the major premise. If a dilemma violates the first rule (if the consequents in the major premise do not follow legitimately from the antecedents) then the appropriate way to respond to the dilemma is to **_grasp it by the horns_**. Grasping the horns involves questioning the truth of either one of the conditional statements in the major premise.

Let's take an example of a dilemma that violates Rule #1 and grasp it by the horns. Let's take the example we used for simple destructive dilemmas:

> If I am to be happy, then I must please both God and men
> But either I must displease God (by pleasing man), or I must displease men (by pleasing God)
> Therefore, I cannot be happy

In grasping a dilemma by the horns, we attack one of the conditional statements in the major premise. Let's attack the second horn, *If I am to be happy, then I must please men.* (Notice that the two conditional statements in the major premise are sort of tangled together. We merely untangled them.)

We must (if we remember the truth conditions of conditional statements) be able to establish that the antecedent is true and the consequent false. In this case we could claim that it is entirely possible to be happy (affirming the antecedent) and not please men (denying the consequent). You could come up with examples of this from history of men who please God (but not men) and were quite happy.

_____ Escaping Between the Horns of a Dilemma. If the dilemma violates Rule #2—that the disjunction in the minor premise must be complete, then we must deal with it by slipping between the horns. This method avoids the necessity of having to question the truth of either of the two conditional statements in the major premise by attacking, instead, the disjunctive statement in the minor premise. This is done by proposing that there is some other alternative than the two offered in the disjunction, thereby avoiding the conclusion.

Let's take Jesus' dilemma again:

> Either Jesus will urge that the woman caught in adultery be stoned or he will urge that she be pardoned
> But if Jesus urges that the woman caught in adultery be stoned, he will be unpopular with the people because of his severity; and if he urges that she be pardoned, then he will be criticized by the Pharisees for disregarding the law of Moses
> Therefore, either Jesus will be unpopular with the people for his severity or he will be criticized by the Pharisees for disregarding the law of Moses

The rule violated (if any) will determine the approach an opponent takes to refuting a dilemma.

What, in fact, did Jesus do? According to the gospel of Mark, he neither urged that the woman be stoned nor that she be pardoned. Instead, he did a third thing. He said, "Let he who is without sin cast the first stone." In this way, Jesus escaped between the horns of the dilemma.

_____ **The Counter-Dilemma.** If the dilemma violates Rule #3— that the conclusion must be exclusive (in other words, it should be the only one that can be inferred from the premises)—then we must deal with it by suggesting a ***counter-dilemma***. The counter-dilemma is one of the most sophisticated and clever operations in logic. It is accomplished by rearranging the propositions in the original dilemma to produce a very different conclusion. Unlike other methods of responding to dilemmas, this method does not question the truth of any of the argument's component propositions nor does it suggest any third alternatives not included in the premises. It is not, therefore, a direct refutation of a dilemma. It merely points out that there is another conclusion that can be derived from the same truths assumed in the premises.

Let's take a look back at the dilemma proposed by Protagoras:

Euthlus must either win the case or lose it
If Euthlus loses his case, then he should pay me (because the court will have decided
    against him); and if Euthlus wins the case, then he should pay me (in accordance with
    our original agreement)
Therefore, in either case, he should pay me

Technically, this dilemma violates Rule #3, since the conclusion is not exhaustive—it does not exhaust the possibilities of what may be concluded. Therefore, a counter-dilemma may be offered. In fact, it is said that Euthlus, in response to Protagoras, did indeed propose a counter-dilemma, showing that Protagoras had taught him well. Here is Euthlus' response:

I must either win the case or lose it
If I win the case, then I should not have to pay Protagorus on account of the judge's ruling
(that I shouldn't have to pay); and if I lose the case, then I shouldn't have to pay it according
to our original agreement (that I would pay only when I won my first case)
Therefore, in either case, I should not have to pay

Notice that, from the same set of truths, Protagoras and Euthlus come to completely different conclusions. The force of the counter-dilemma is to show that your opponent's conclusion is not the only one that can follow from the truths he states: that another truth or set of truths (more favorable to your side) is consistent with these truths.

The counter-dilemma is one of the most sophisticated and clever operations in logic.

But how is this done? There are two ways to do it depending on whether the dilemma is constructive or destructive.

> **Procedure #1:** If the dilemma is **constructive**, then the **consequents** of the major premise may be switched and negated
>
> **Procedure #2:** If the dilemma is **destructive**, then the **antecedents** of the major premise may be switched and negated

In the case of Euthlus, since it was a constructive dilemma, the first procedure was followed:

The Original:

and negate
If P, then Q; and if R, then S
and negate

Either P or R

Therefore, either Q or S
and negate
and negate

Is changed to:

If P, then **not** S; and if R, then **not** Q

Either P or R

Therefore, either **not** S or **not** Q

Transposition of the two terms in the conclusion is not really necessary, since transposing disjuncts does not affect the statement logically. It just makes it look cleaner.

A counter-dilemma involving a destructive dilemma would look like this:

The Original:

and negate
If P, then Q; and if R, then S
and negate
Either **not** Q or **not** S

Therefore, either **not** P or **not** R
and negate
and negate

Is changed to:

If **not** R, then Q; and if **not** P, then S

Either **not** Q or **not** S

Therefore, either R or P

In the case of both constructive and destructive dilemmas, if the dilemma is simple, switching the terms in the conclusion is unnecessary (since there is only one term in the conclusion), but negation must still be performed. Remember also that a counter-dilemma is an option only when Rule #3 is violated.

In destructive dilemmas, if the dilemma is simple, switching the terms is unnecessary, but negation must still be performed.

_____ **Summary.** A dilemma is an argument which presents, as the major premise, a complex conjunctive proposition in which each of the conjuncts is a conditional statement, as well as a minor premise, a disjunctive proposition, in which either the antecedents of the major premise are alternatively confirmed, or its consequents denied.

The dilemma takes four forms:

- ✓ The simple constructive dilemma
- ✓ The simple destructive dilemma
- ✓ The complex constructive dilemma
- ✓ The complex destructive dilemma

There are three rules for dilemmas:

Rule #1 (concerning the *major premise*): The consequents in the major premise must follow legitimately from the antecedents (in other words, the major premise must be true)

Rule #2 (concerning the *minor premise*): The disjunction in the minor premise must be complete (in other words, there must be no third possibility)

Rule #3 (concerning the *conclusion*): The conclusion must be exclusive (in other words, it should be the only one that can be inferred from the premises)

Depending on which of these rules a dilemma violates, there are three ways of responding to them:

Response #1: Grasping by the horns (if there is a violation of Rule #1)

Response #2: Escaping between the horns (if there is a violation of Rule #2)

Response #3: Counter-dilemma (if there is a violation of Rule #3)

_____ **Exercises for Day I. Peruse entire chapter. Then read section titled, "What is a Dilemma?" Read this section carefully and try to understand it as best you can.**

1. What is a dilemma?

2. How many forms does the dilemma take?

3. How many rules for the dilemma are there?

4. How many strategies are there for responding to dilemmas?

Read section titled, "The Classification of Dilemmas." Read it carefully.

5. How are dilemmas divided *quantitatively*?

6. How are dilemmas divided *qualitatively*?

7. Taking both quantity and quality into account, list the possible forms of the dilemma.

Read section titled, "The Simple Constructive Dilemma." Read it carefully.

8. Explain what a simple constructive dilemma is.

9. Give the form of a simple constructive dilemma.

10. With the form in mind, construct a simple dilemma using the following component propositions:

    P=Socrates dies when he is living
    Q=Socrates cannot be dead
    R=Socrates dies when he is dead

Read section titled, "The Simple Destructive Dilemma." Read it carefully.

11. Explain what a simple destructive dilemma is.

12. Give the form of a simple destructive dilemma.

13. With this form in mind, construct a simple destructive dilemma using the following component propositions:

    P=a thing moves
    Q=it moves in the place where it is
    R=it moves in the place where it is not

_____ **Exercises for Day 2. Read section titled, "The Complex Constructive Dilemma." Read it carefully.**

14. Explain what a complex constructive dilemma is.

15. Give the form of a complex constructive dilemma.

16. With this form in mind, construct a complex constructive dilemma using the following component propositions:

> P=in this life, we obey our vicious inclinations
> Q=we will bring sin and sorrow
> R=in this life, we resist our vicious inclinations
> S=we will experience labor and pain

Read section titled, "The Complex Destructive Dilemma." Read it carefully.

17. Explain what a complex destructive dilemma is.

18. Give the form of a complex destructive dilemma.

19. With this form in mind, construct a complex destructive dilemma using the following component propositions:

> P=we are to be happy in this life
> Q=we must follow our desires
> R=we are to be happy in the life hereafter
> S=we must restrain our desires

Read section titled, "Rules for the Dilemma." Read it carefully.

20. List the three rules for dilemmas and explain them in your own words.

21. What does the violation of any one of these rules help to determine?

22. Determine whether the simple constructive dilemma you constructed in question 10 complies with these rules. Indicate which, if any, of these rules it violates. If it violates any rule, reformulate it so that it complies.

23. Determine whether the simple destructive dilemma you constructed in question 13 complies with these rules. Indicate which, if any, of these rules it violates. If it violates any rule, reformulate it so that it complies.

24. Determine whether the complex constructive dilemma you constructed in question 16 complies with these rules. Indicate which, if any, of these rules it violates. If it violates any rule, reformulate it so that it complies.

25. Determine whether the complex destructive dilemma you constructed in question 19 complies with these rules. Indicate which, if any, of these rules it violates. If it violates any rule, reformulate it so that it complies.

_____ **Exercises for Day 3.**

26. In the early days of the Christian Church, there were a number of disputes that took place over the nature of Christ. One of them involved whether or not He was capable of sinning. In one camp were those who believed He was able to sin but did not; in other words He was *potuit non peccare*: able not to sin. In the other camp were those who held that He was not able to sin at all; in other words, that he was *non potuit peccare*: not able to sin. This created the dilemma which follows. Tell which kind of dilemma it is an example of:

> If Jesus was able to sin, then he could not have been God; if he was not able to sin, then he could not be man. But he is either able to sin or not able to sin. Therefore, he was either not God or not man.

Read section titled, "Grasping the Dilemma by the Horns." Read it carefully.

27. Grasping a dilemma by the horns is suggested by the violation of what rule?

28. What is involved in grasping a dilemma by the horns?

29. Look back at your answers to questions 10, 13, 16 and 19. If any of them violates the relevant rule, then grasp it by the horns.

30. Grasp the dilemma in question 26 by the horns.

31. There are many people who profess to be moral relativists; that is, they maintain that there are no moral absolutes that exist as standards outside of and governing all of us. They can be refuted with this dilemma, which shows that their argument is self-defeating. Identify the kind of dilemma of which it is an example:

> Either moral standards are absolute or they are not. If morality is absolute, then there is at least one thing that is absolute; namely, moral standards. If moral standards are not absolute, then there is at least one thing that is absolute; namely the belief that there are no absolutes. In either case, there is at least one thing that is absolute.

Read section titled, "Escaping Between the Horns of a Dilemma." Read it carefully.

32. Escaping between the horns of a dilemma is suggested by the violation of what rule?

33. What is involved in escaping between the horns of a dilemma?

34. Look back at your answers to questions 10, 13, 16, and 19. If any of them violates the relevant rule, then escape between the horns.

35. In Plato's *Meno*, Socrates argues that all knowledge is really recollection; in other words, we never really learn anything new, but only recollect that which we knew in the life our soul led before being born. This is why Socrates always questioned his listeners: because he believed learning was a matter of recollection, not instruction. His argument is in the form of a dilemma.

Identify what kind of dilemma this is:

Either then, [man] has at some time acquired the knowledge which he now has, or he has always possessed it. If he always possessed it, he must always have known; if on the other hand he acquired it at some previous time, it cannot have been in this life, unless somebody has taught him geometry. He will behave in the same way with all geometric knowledge, and every other subject. Has anyone taught him all these?

Read section titled, "The Counter-Dilemma." Read it carefully.

36. A counter-dilemma is suggested by the violation of what rule?

37. How is the counter-dilemma different from other methods of responding to dilemmas?

38. Explain generally, in your own words, how a counter-dilemma works.

39. Explain specifically how each of the two procedures for counter-dilemmas work.

40. Show by using the symbols A, B and C how a counter-dilemma for a simple constructive dilemma is performed. (Show the original dilemma and the counter-dilemma.)

41. Show by using the symbols A, B and C how a counter-dilemma for a simple destructive dilemma is performed. (Show the original dilemma and the counter-dilemma.)

42. Show by using the symbols A, B, C and D how a counter-dilemma for a complex constructive dilemma is performed. (Show the original dilemma and the counter-dilemma.)

43. Show by using the symbols A, B, C and D how a counter-dilemma for a complex destructive dilemma is performed. (Show the original dilemma and the counter-dilemma.)

44. Look back at your answers to questions 10, 13, 16 and 19. If any of them violates the relevant rule, then create a counter-dilemma in response to it.

_____ **Exercises for Day 4.**

45. The following argument was offered by St. Augustine as showing that Christianity was of God. Identify the kind of dilemma it is by writing out the form:

Christianity spread throughout the world either by miracles or not. If by miracles, then it is of God, for otherwise He would not have worked miracles in its favor; if not by miracles, then it is also of God, since the incredible spread of Christianity without miracles is itself a miracle. Therefore, in either case, Christianity is of God.

46. Tertullian criticized the policy of Emperors Trajan and Marcus Aurelius in regard to the persecution of Christians. The policy was a sort of "don't ask, don't tell" policy in which quiet Christians could not be pursued, but if their faith was somehow made public, then they could be persecuted. Identify the kind of dilemma it is by writing out the form:

Either Christians have committed crimes or they have not. If they have committed crimes, then there should be no restrictions on hunting them down. If they have not committed crimes, then you should not punish them when they are brought to your attention. Therefore, in either case, your policy is unjust.

47. Offer a counter-dilemma to the following argument:

Either Fate has determined that I die today or it has not. If fate has determined that I die today, then it is useless to avoid danger; if fate has not determined that I die today, then avoiding danger is unnecessary. Therefore, it is either futile or unnecessary for me to avoid danger today.

48. The following is the historical dilemma called the "Dilemma of Caliph Omar", who offered the following dilemma to justify the burning of the library of Alexandria in 640 A. D. Attack either one or both of the horns of this dilemma:

If the books in the library of Alexandria are in conformity with the Koran, then they are superfluous (and should be burned); and if the books in the library of Alexandria are not in conformity with the Koran, then they are pernicious (and should be burned)
Either the books in the library of Alexandria are in conformity with the Koran or they are not.
Therefore, either they are superfluous or they are pernicious (and should be burned).

49. Devise a counter-dilemma for the following dilemma:

If you tell the truth, you will make men unhappy; if you tell lies, you will risk the wrath of God. Either you will tell the truth or tell lies. Therefore, you will either make men unhappy or you will risk the wrath of God.

Read section titled, "Summary." Read it carefully.

50. Indicate whether the following are true or false:

T	F	A dilemma is an argument which presents, as the major premise, a conjunctive proposition in which each of the conjuncts is a conditional statement, as well as a minor premise, a disjunctive proposition, in which either the consequents of the major premise are confirmed, or its antecedents denied.
T	F	The four forms a dilemma takes are as follows: simple constructive, simple destructive, complex constructive and complex destructive.
T	F	According to Rule #2 for dilemmas, the disjunction in the major premise must be complete.
T	F	There are three ways of responding to dilemmas.
T	F	The counter-dilemma is not a direct refutation of a dilemma.
T	F	The violation of one of the three rules for dilemmas will determine which method of response is used.

_____ **Weekly Analysis Assignment. Find an article from a newspaper (letters to the editor in newspapers are ideal) or magazine or a chapter from a book you are reading that contains a dilemma or make up your own using the forms that you have studied. If you are able to find one, either write a short 1-2 page essay or make a presentation in class analyzing the argument. The paper or presentation should contain the following elements:**

1. A *presentation* of the argument as it was originally written.
2. A *summary* of the argument in your own words.
3. An *analysis* of the logical form of the argument.
4. An *evaluation* of the argument's soundness. This will involve assessing both the truth of the argument's premises and its validity. Remember that if the argument is valid and the premises are true, the conclusion must be true. If the argument is valid and one or more of the premises are false, then the conclusion must also be false. And if the argument is invalid, the truth of the conclusion cannot be determined one way or another by knowing the truth of the premises.
5. State your agreement or disagreement with the argument you have analyzed.

DAVID HUME

The Problem of Evil

_____The Argument in Plain Language: "If God is good, then why do bad things happen to good people?"

_____The Argument: "And is it possible, CLEANTHES, said PHILO, that after all these reflections, and infinitely more, which might be suggested, you can still persevere in your Anthropomorphism, and assert the moral attributes of the Deity, his justice, benevolence, mercy, and rectitude, to be of the same nature with these virtues in human creatures? His power we allow is infinite: whatever he wills is executed: but neither man nor any other animal is happy: therefore he does not will their happiness. His wisdom is infinite: He is never mistaken in choosing the means to any end: But the course of Nature tends not to human or animal felicity: therefore it is not established for that purpose. Through the whole compass of human knowledge, there are no inferences more certain and infallible than these. In what respect, then, do his benevolence and mercy resemble the benevolence and mercy of men? EPICURUS's old questions are yet unanswered: *Is [God] willing to prevent evil, but not able? then is he impotent. Is he able, but not willing? then is he malevolent. Is he both able and willing? whence then is evil?*"
—**David Hume, *Dialogues Concerning Natural Religion*, Part X**

_____ Background of the Argument: David Hume, a British empirical philospher of the 18th century, was a notorious sceptic. This classic statement of the problem of evil was uttered by Hume in one of his two famous attacks on religious belief (another was his attack on the possibility of miracles.) Hume uses this argument in order to further undermine religious belief in general, and the belief in the existence of God in particular. The oldest presentation of the argument, however, is in the Old Testament book of Job. God allows Job to be tested by Satan, and Job is visited with great suffering. His friends tell him that he is being punished for some evil he has done, but this cannot be, since even God says that Job is a good man. He cries out to God for an answer, and God comes to him out of the whirlwind. God does not answer Job, but instead asks Job questions he cannot answer. Forced now to answer the questions of his Creator, Job realizes his mistake in daring to question God. Humbled by His presence, Job prostrates himself before Him, and repents, saying, "You asked, 'Who is this who hides counsel without knowledge?' Therefore I have uttered what I did not understand ... Therefore I abhor myself, and repent in dust and ashes." "The riddles of God," said G. K. Chesterton, "are more satisfying than the solutions of man."

_____ Assignment:
1. Put the argument into the proper form of a dilemma.
2. Write a short, 2-3 page essay evaluating the argument. Explain how the argument can be refuted using the most appropriate of the three methods of responding to a dilemma.
3. Write a short, 1-3 page biographical essay on David Hume.

The Oblique Syllogism

_____ **The Oblique Syllogism.** The last kind of syllogism we will discuss is called the *oblique* syllogism. It gets its name from the fact that one of its terms is in an oblique case—i.e. a case other than the nominative (the case of the subject). In normal categorical syllogisms, all the terms are in the nominative case. The oblique syllogism is similar to a categorical syllogism, but with a twist. In a normal categorical syllogism, a major term is identified with a minor term by means of a third (or middle) term. In an oblique syllogism, however, a middle term is **not** the means of identification between the major and minor terms. Instead, a certain *relation* between the major and minor terms is inferred. Here is an example:

> Peter^M is a philosopher^P
> This man^S is ***the son of***_r Peter^M
> Therefore, this man^S is ***the son of***_r a philosopher^P

It has the following form:

> M is P
> S is M_r
> S is P_r

Notice that you still have a major, minor and middle term, but that there is another element to the argument: *r*. This term—*r*—stands for the relation that is being inferred between *man*, the minor term, and *philosopher*, the major term.

_____ **The Validity of Oblique Syllogisms.** If a person did not know how an oblique syllogism worked, he would want to say that this syllogism has more than three terms, and therefore commits a fallacy. However, a fallacy is not necessarily committed here because the rules are somewhat different. For one thing, the middle term does not need to be distributed in the argument, since it is not the means by which the

In oblique syllogisms, a certain relation is inferred between the major and minor term.

two terms are identified. However, *the same rules apply to the major and minor terms as in a normal categorical syllogism*.

In oblique syllogisms the validity depends, not on whether the middle term is distributed, but on whether there is a legitimate *transitive relationship* between the relevant terms. A transitive relationship is a relationship that can be transferred from one set of concepts to another. In the case of our previous example, that relationship is the condition of being *the son of*, which is transferred from *Peter* to *a philosopher*.

Contrast the previous oblique syllogism with the following:

> All tyrants are men
> Adolf Hitler was the world's greatest tyrant
> Therefore, Adolf Hitler was the world's greatest man

In this case, the *world's greatest* simply does not indicate a transitive relationship; it is intransitive. Being the *world's greatest tyrant* does not translate into being the *world's greatest man*, even though Adolf Hitler was a man. In the previous oblique syllogism, the *son of* relationship was transitive. Being the *son of Peter* translates into being the *son of a philosopher*, since Peter is a philosopher.

There is no *formal* reason why this is so, rather, it is a *material* relation. While in formal reasoning, the question of whether one thing follows from another is dependent merely on the *form* of the reasoning, the validity of the oblique syllogism can spring from either its form or *the special character of the content* of the argument. In other words, the validity of categorical and hypothetical arguments is unaffected by the content of the argument, while, in oblique syllogisms, the validity is determined both by its form and by its content.

We include a study of them in our overall analysis of the formal syllogism because many of their characteristics are syllogistic in nature.

_____ *A Fortiori* **Arguments.** There is one class of arguments which, technically, are formally invalid, but which, nevertheless, contain conclusions that obviously follow from the premises. These are called *a fortiori* arguments. An example would be the following:

> A is greater than B
> B is greater than C
> Therefore, A is greater than C

_____ **Summary.** An oblique syllogism is a syllogism in which it is a *relation*, not a middle term, that connects the minor to the major terms. In oblique syllogisms the validity depends, not on whether the middle term is distributed, but on whether it meets the rules that apply to the major and minor terms as well as whether there is a legitimate *transitive relationship* between the relevant terms. The transitivity, however, is a relation of *material logic* rather than of formal logic.

One common class of arguments is called *a fortiori* arguments. These are formally invalid, but their conclusions obviously follow from the premises.

A *fortiori* **arguments are technically invalid, yet their conclusions obviously follow from the premises.**

_____ **Exercises for Day 1.** **Peruse entire chapter. Then read the section titled, "The Oblique Syllogism." Read this section carefully and try to understand it as best you can.**

1. Where does the oblique syllogism get its name?

2. In what way is it different from a standard categorical syllogism?

3. What does the term *r* stand for in an oblique syllogism?

Read section titled, "Validity of Oblique Syllogisms." Read it carefully.

4. If you were to treat the oblique syllogism as if it were a standard syllogism, what fallacy would you say it committed?

5. Why does the middle term not need to be distributed?

6. On what does the validity of the oblique syllogism depend?

7. In what way is the source of the validity of an oblique syllogism different from that of a categorical syllogism?

8. Put each of the following into the form of a valid oblique syllogism if possible. Tell why you think each is valid or invalid:

America is a great country. I am an American citizen. Therefore, I am the citizen of a great country.

Television viewing is mindless activity. This man is an advocate of television viewing. Therefore, this man is an advocate of mindless activity.

Public schooling is a corrupt system. My child is a product of public schooling. Therefore, my child is a product of a corrupt system.

Peter is a man. Men are the product of creation. Therefore, Peter is a product of creation.

Breaking the speed limit is a crime. Crime is a result of family breakdown. Therefore, breaking the speed limit is the result of family breakdown.

_____ **Exercises for Day 2.** **Read the section titled, "A Fortiori Arguments." Read the entire section carefully.**

9. What makes *a fortiori* arguments unique?

10. Create an *a fortiori* argument that is similar in structure to the one presented in the text, but using the symbols (P, Q and R).

11. Put the following *a fortiori* syllogisms into proper logical form:

Communism is worse than Naziism and Naziism is worse than dictatorship. Therefore, communism is worse than dictatorship.

Peter is taller than Paul and Paul is taller than Mary. Therefore, Peter is taller than Mary.

A square has a greater number of sides than a triangle, and a pentagon has a greater number of sides than a square. Therefore, a pentagon has a greater number of sides than a triangle.

Socrates is smarter than Plato and Plato is smarter than Aristotle. Therefore, Socrates is smarter than Aristotle.

Americans are freer than Russians and Russians are freer than Chinese. Therefore, Americans are freer than Chinese.

12. Tell whether the following oblique syllogisms are valid or invalid. If they are invalid, indicate whether they are formally invalid or materially invalid:

All communists are Marxists. Stalin was the most evil communist of all. Therefore, Stalin was the most evil Marxist of all.

Peter is a banker. Paul is Peter's attorney. Therefore, Paul is a banker's attorney.

Mary is my children's aunt. I only have two children. Therefore, Mary is the aunt of only two children.

All philosophers are thinkers. Socrates was the greatest philosopher. Therefore, Socrates was the greatest thinker.

My self-esteem is dependent upon my relationship with God. My relationship with God is intangible. Therefore, my self-esteem is dependent upon an intangible.

The right to bear arms is guaranteed by the Constitution. All infringements of the right to bear arms are unjust. Therefore, all unjust acts are infringements of rights guaranteed under the Constitution.

Our destiny is determined by God. God is love. Therefore, our destiny is determined by love.

_____ **Exercises for Day 3.**
Construct your own valid oblique syllogisms in the following moods:

13. BARBARA

14. CELARENT

15. CESARE

16. CAMESTRES

17. CAMENES

18. Reduce the oblique syllogisms not based on First Figure arguments in questions 13-17 into First Figure arguments.

_____ **Exercises for Day 4.** **Read section titled, "Summary." Read it carefully.**

19. Construct three *a fortiori* syllogisms of your own.

20. Put the *a fortiori* arguments you construced in question 19 into proper logical form.

21. Tell whether the following are true or false:

T	F	In oblique syllogisms, the minor term determines validity.
T	F	In oblique syllogisms, validity depends, in part on a transitive relationship.
T	F	Technically speaking, *a fortiori* arguments are invalid.

_____ **Weekly Analysis Assignment.** **Find an article from a newspaper (letters to the editor in newspapers are ideal) or magazine or a chapter from a book you are reading that contains oblique reasoning or that contains an *a fortiori* argument. Either write a short 1-2 page essay or make a presentation in class analyzing the argument. The paper or presentation should contain the following elements:**

1. A *presentation* of the argument as it was originally written.
2. A *summary* of the argument in your own words.
3. An *analysis* of the logical form of the argument.
4. An *evaluation* of the argument's soundness. This will involve assessing both the truth of the argument's premises and its validity. Remember that if the argument is valid and the premises are true, the conclusion must be true. If the argument is valid and one or more of the premises are false, then the conclusion must also be false. And if the argument is invalid, the truth of the conclusion cannot be determined one way or another by knowing the truth of the premises.
5. State your agreement or disagreement with the argument you have analyzed.

Mary

Is Mary the Mother of God?

_____**The Argument in Plain Language:** "If Mary is the mother of Jesus, then she is the Mother of God."

_____**The Argument:** "...the Lord Jesus Christ is God. But if He is God, as He certainly is, then she who bore God is the Mother of God."
—**John Cassian,** *On the Incarnation of Christ Against the Nestorians,* **429 A. D.**

_____ **Background of the Argument:** The debate over this argument has a long and storied history. Although it is often cast as a debate between Catholics and Protestants, that is very much an oversimplification. In fact, although the belief that Mary is the Mother of God is often thought to be a peculiarly Catholic belief, it has had many Protestant adherents, including all of the great reformers, including Martin Luther, John Calvin, Philipp Melancthon and Ulrich Zwingli, as well as more modern Protestant thinkers such as R. C. Sproul. Most modern Protestants, however, have spurned the belief, grouping it with other Catholic beliefs about Mary that Protestants see as crossing the line between a reverence for Mary and a worship of her. Catholics point to the logic of the argument, the form of which is a classic oblique syllogism; Protestants, on the other hand, claim the belief cannot be justifed from the Scriptures. In the early history of the Church, Christian leaders such as John Cassian saw the questioning of the belief that Mary was the Mother of God as a means of ultimately calling the doctrine of the Incarnation into question. They believed that in saying that Mary was only the Mother of Christ, not the Mother of God, that Jesus' personhood (fully God and fully man in the same person) was being called into question. They saw this as a heresy and condemned it. Today, this heresy seems a distant thing, but the doctrine formulated to deal with it continues to stir controversy among Christians.

_____ **Assignment:**
1. Try to summarize the argument in one simple syllogism. Remember that it is an oblique syllogism. Determine whether it is valid or invalid.
2. Research the Nestorian Heresy and say whether you think the argument is sound. Give your reasons why or why not. Write a short essay or make a presentation justifying your conclusions.

Chapter 15

"There is nothing in this world except a syllogism—and a fallacy."

—**G. K. Chesterton**

Review Exercises

for Book II

_____ **Exercises for Day I.** **Read summary sections in chapters 1-4 as needed to answer the true/false questions.**

1. Tell whether the following are true or false:

T	F	We label a First Figure syllogism *sub-prae*.
T	F	The Third Figure is really just a form of the First Figure.
T	F	*Prae-prae* is short for the Latin *praedicatum-praedicatum*.
T	F	In a syllogism of the Second Figure, the major term is the subject in the major premise and the predicate of the minor premise.
T	F	The figure of a syllogism is the disposition of terms in the conclusion.
T	F	The Fourth Figure is sometimes called the Galenic figure.
T	F	Mood is the disposition of terms in a syllogism.
T	F	The mood of a syllogism of the form CELARENT is EA.
T	F	There are sixteen moods per figure.
T	F	There are sixteen valid moods.
T	F	BARBARA, CELARENT, DARII and FERIO are valid syllogisms of the First Figure.
T	F	Syllogisms in the mood OO are always invalid.
T	F	There are four operations by which syllogisms can be reduced to the first figure.
T	F	The consonants S, P, M and C, when found in the body of the name of a syllogism, indicate which figure the syllogism is in.
T	F	The consonant S indicates simple conversion of the proposition signified by the preceding vowel.
T	F	M indicates one of the methods of Direct Reduction.
T	F	C indicates one of the methods of Indirect Reduction.
T	F	M indicates that the reduction of the syllogism must be done in multiple steps.
T	F	Syllogisms in the Fourth (or Indirect First) Figure cannot be reduced to the First Figure.
T	F	The two moods in which Direct Reduction does not work are BARBARA and BAROCO.
T	F	In those cases in which Direct Reduction cannot be used, we must use Indirect Reduction.
T	F	The reason we reduce figures to the First is in order to more easily show them valid.
T	F	We indirectly reduce a syllogism by replacing the O premise with the contradiction of the original conclusion.
T	F	In Indirect Reduction, if the contradiction of the major premise also contradicts the contradiction of the minor premise, then the syllogism contradicts itself.

Alice in Wonderland
by Lewis Carroll

2. This passage illustrates a terminological problem that is at the root of one of the terminological fallacies discussed in Chapter 11 of Book I. What is the relevant fallacy?

The next thing was to eat the comfits: this caused some noise and confusion, as the large birds complained that they could not taste theirs, and the small ones choked and had to be patted on the back. However, it was over at last, and they sat down again in a ring, and begged the Mouse to tell them something more.

'You promised to tell me your history, you know,' said Alice, 'and why it is you hate—C and D,' she added in a whisper, half afraid that it would be offended again.

'Mine is a long and a sad tale!' said the Mouse, turning to Alice and sighing.

'It *is* a long tail,' certainly,' said Alice, looking down with wonder at the Mouse's tail; 'but why do you call it sad?"

3. The following passage displays a valid argument form. Tell what the valid argument form is and write it out in proper logical form:

> Alice noticed with some surprise that the pebbles were all turning into little cakes as they lay on the floor, and a bright idea came into her head. 'If I eat one of these cakes,' she thought, 'it's sure to make some change in my size; and, as it can't possibly make me larger, it must make me smaller, I suppose.'

4. Here is another argument form which, in this case, illustrates a fallacy. State the argument in proper logical form and indicate what fallacy is committed.

> 'I—I'm a little girl,' said Alice, rather doubtfully, as she remembered the number of changes she had gone through, that day.
> 'A likely story indeed!' said the Pigeon in a tone of the deepest contempt. 'I've seen a good many little girls in my time, but never one with such a neck as that! No, no! You're a serpent; and there's no use denying it. I suppose you'll be telling me next that you never tasted an egg!'
> 'I have tasted eggs, certainly,' said Alice, who was a very truthful child; 'but little girls eat eggs quite as much as serpents do, you know.'
> 'I don't believe it,' said the Pigeon; 'but if they do, why, then, they're a kind of serpent, that's all I can say.'

_____ **Daily Exercises for Day 2.** Read summary sections in chapters 5-8 as needed to answer the true/false questions.

5. Tell whether the following are true or false:

T	F	A quantifier is a form of the *to be* verb.
T	F	The complement is a word that links together a subject and a predicate.
T	F	Exclusive sentences should be changed into A statements.
T	F	An exceptive statement needs only a complement.
T	F	The word *all* is a quantifier.
T	F	An enthymeme is the most common argument form.
T	F	All enthymemes are missing a conclusion.
T	F	A Third Order enthymeme is a syllogism that is missing a minor premise.
T	F	Enthymemes are missing one statement in the argument because the statement is logically unnecessary for the argument to be valid.
T	F	There are four valid moods of conditional syllogisms.
T	F	One of the invalid moods is called the *Fallacy of Affirming the Antecedent*.
T	F	A conditional syllogism and a conjunctive syllogism are both hypothetical syllogisms.
T	F	The major premise in a hypothetical syllogism is the premise which contains the major term.
T	F	The consequent is the proposition in a conditional statement that appears before the *then*.
T	F	There are four valid moods of disjunctive syllogisms.
T	F	The invalid moods are all *tollendo ponens*.
T	F	A conditional syllogism and a disjunctive syllogism are both hypothetical syllogisms.
T	F	The major premise in a disjunctive syllogism is the premise which contains the major term.
T	F	The alternant is the proposition of a disjunctive statement that appears only in the conclusion.
T	F	A disjunctive statement in which one alternant is true and the other false is a false statement.

William Shakespeare

6. In this passage from Shakespeare's *Henry IV*, Falstaff is defending himself against Prince Henry's denunciation. Put the following argument in proper form and indicate if the form is valid (the italicized part is the relevant section):

> If sack and sugar be a fault, God help the wicked! *If to be old and merry be a sin, then many an old host that I know is damned.*

7. In this passage from *Troilus and Cressida*, Shakespeare puts in the mouth of Ulysses an argument that social hierarchy is necessary if anarchy is to be avoided. It is one of the complex syllogisms we have studied. Identify the type of syllogism it is, put it in its proper logical form, and indicate whether it is valid and why:

> Force should be right, or, rather, right and wrong—
> Between whose endless jar justice resides—
> Should lose their names, and so justice too.
> Then everything includes itself in power,
> Power into will, will into appetite;
> And appetite, an universal wolf,
> So doubly seconded with will and power,
> Must make perforce an universal prey,
> And last eat up himself.

8. Here is another Shakespeare passage, this from *Much Ado about Nothing,* containing a complex argument. See if you can identify the kind of argument it is, put it in proper logical form and indicate whether you think it is valid:

> He that hath a beard is more than a youth, and he that hath no beard is less than a man; and he that is more than a youth is not for me, and he that is less than a man, I am not for him.

_____ **Exercises for Day 3.** **Read Summary sections in chapters 9-12 as needed to answer the true/false questions.**

9. Tell whether the following are true or false:

T	F	There are four valid moods of conjunctive syllogisms.
T	F	All of the invalid moods are *ponendo tollens*.
T	F	A conjunctive syllogism and a disjunctive syllogism are both hypothetical syllogisms.
T	F	The major premise in a conjunctive syllogism is the premise which contains the major term.
T	F	The conjunct is the proposition of a disjunctive statement that appears only in the conclusion.
T	F	There are four kinds of complex syllogisms: polysyllogisms, epicheirema, Aristotelian sorites and Goclenian sorites.
T	F	A *polysyllogism* is a syllogism that links together several syllogisms in such a way that the conclusion of one syllogism serves as a premise in the next one.
T	F	The *sorites* is a chain argument which, through a chain of premises (without the intermediate conclusions), connects the predicate of the first premise with the subject of the conclusion.
T	F	There are two kinds of sorites: the *Aristotelian* and the *Galenic*.

T	F	The Aristotelian sorites is a series of Fourth (or Indirect First) Figure syllogisms with all of the conclusions unexpressed except the last.
T	F	There are two kinds of sorites: affirmative and negative.
T	F	Goclenian sorites are similar to the Aristotelian, except that the series of syllogisms are **First Figure** rather than **Fourth**.
T	F	The validity of Goclenian sorites depends on the validity of the component syllogisms of which it is comprised.
T	F	There are five valid forms of conditional sorites.
T	F	Epicheirema are syllogisms in which at least one of the premises contains a causal proposition.
T	F	A causal proposition is a proposition which is the proof for another proposition or the reason for believing the other proposition to be false.
T	F	First Order epicheirema are epicheirema in which the causal proposition is in the minor premise.
T	F	Third Order epicheirema are similar to Aristotelian sorites.
T	F	In order to check the validity of epicheirema, we must first extrapolate them.
T	F	Like Aristotelian sorites, it is the minor premise in Second Order epicheirema that must be extrapolated.

I Corinthians 15:12-22
St. Paul

10. The epistles of St. Paul are a rich source of arguments, mostly (since Paul is using ordinary language) in the form of enthymemes. Any syllogistic or hypothetical argument form can be stated in the form of an enthymeme, and Paul makes use of numerous forms in his discussion of Christian doctrine. Here Paul uses several argument forms conjoined together in a complex formation. Try to identify as many of the simple arguments as you can and indicate as many of the larger complex arguments (of which the simple ones may be a part) as you can. Identify them, and put them in proper logical form.

¹²Now if Christ be preached that he rose from the dead, how say some among you that there is no resurrection of the dead?

¹³But if there be no resurrection of the dead, then is Christ not risen:

¹⁴And if Christ be not risen, then is our preaching vain, and your faith is also vain.

¹⁵Yea, and we are found false witnesses of God; because we have testified of God that he raised up Christ: whom he raised not up, if so be that the dead rise not.

¹⁶For if the dead rise not, then is not Christ raised:

¹⁷And if Christ be not raised, your faith is vain; ye are yet in your sins.

¹⁸Then they also which are fallen asleep in Christ are perished.

¹⁹If in this life only we have hope in Christ, we are of all men most miserable.

²⁰But now is Christ risen from the dead, and become the firstfruits of them that slept.

²¹For since by man came death, by man came also the resurrection of the dead.

²²For as in Adam all die, even so in Christ shall all be made alive.

_____ **Exercises for Day 4.** **Read summary sections in chapters 13 and 14 as needed to answer the true/false questions.**

11. Tell whether the following are true or false:

T	F	A dilemma is an argument which presents, as the major premise, a conjunctive proposition in which each of the conjuncts is a conditional statement, as well as a minor premise, a disjunctive proposition, in which either the consequents of the major premise are confirmed, or its antecedents denied.

T	F	The four forms a dilemma takes are as follows: simple constructive, simple destructive, complex constructive and complex destructive.
T	F	According to Rule #2 for dilemmas, the disjunction in the major premise must be complete.
T	F	There are three ways of responding to dilemmas.
T	F	The counter-dilemma is not a direct refutation of a dilemma.
T	F	The violation of one of the three rules for dilemmas will determine which method of response is used.
T	F	In oblique syllogisms the minor term determines validity.
T	F	In oblique syllogisms the transitive relationship determines validity.

Summa Theologica

St. Thomas Aquinas

12. The writings of St. Thomas provide probably the most clearly stated examples of syllogistic reasoning ever written. Here Thomas addresses the question of whether saving faith comes ultimately from man himself or from God. Identify at least five argument forms in the three paragraphs that follow "I answer that..." and write them in their proper logical form:

We proceed thus to the Ninth Article:--

Objection 1. It would seem that faith is not infused into man by God. For Augustine says that "science begets faith in us, and nourishes, defends and strengthens it" (*De Trinitate*, xiv, 1). Now those things which science begets in us seem to be acquired rather than infused. Therefore faith does not seem to be in us by divine infusion.

Objection 2. Further, That to which man attains by hearing and seeing seems to be acquired by him. Now man attains to belief both by seeing miracles and by hearing the teachings of faith; for it is written (John 4:53): "The father ... knew that it was at the same hour, that Jesus said to him, Thy son liveth; and himself believed, and his whole house"; and (Rom. 10: 17) it is said that "faith is through hearing." Therefore man attains to faith by acquiring it.

Objection 3. Further, That which depends on a man's will can be acquired by him. But "faith depends on the believer's will," according to Augustine (*De Praedestinatione Sanctorum, V*). Therefore faith can be acquired by man.

On the contrary, It is written, (Eph. 2: 8, 9): "By grace you are saved through faith, and that not of yourselves ... that no man may glory, for it is the gift of God."

I answer that, Two things are requisite for faith. First, that the things which are of faith should be proposed to man; and this is necessary in order that man believe something explicitly. The second thing requisite for faith is the assent of the believer to the things which are proposed to him. Accordingly, as regards the first of these, faith must needs be from God. For the things which are of faith surpass human reason, and hence they do not come to man's knowledge, unless God reveal them. To some, indeed, they are revealed by God immediately, as those things which were revealed to the Apostles and prophets, while to some they are proposed by God in sending preachers of the faith, according to Rom. 10:15: "How shall they preach, unless they be sent?"

As regards the second, viz., man's assent to the things which are of faith, we may observe a twofold cause, one of external inducement, such as seeing a miracle, or being persuaded by someone to embrace the faith; neither of which is a sufficient cause, since of those who see the same miracle, or who hear the same sermon, some believe, and some do not. Hence we must assert another and internal cause, which moves man inwardly to assent to what belongs to faith.

The Pelagians held that this cause was nothing else than man's free choice, and consequently they said that the beginning of faith is from ourselves, inasmuch, namely, it is in our power to be ready to assent to the things which are of faith, but that the consummation of faith is from God, who proposes to us the things we have to believe. But this is false, for since, by assenting to what belongs to faith, man is raised above nature, this must needs come to him from some supernatural principle, moving him inwardly; and this is God. Therefore faith, as regards the assent which is the chief act of faith, is from God moving man inwardly by grace.

Reply Objection 1. Science begets and nourishes faith by way of external persuasion afforded by some science; but the chief and proper cause of faith is that which moves man inwardly to assent.

Reply Objection 2. This argument likewise refers to the cause that proposes outwardly the things that are of faith, or persuades man to believe by words or deeds.

Reply Objection 3. To believe does indeed depend on the will of the believer; but man's will needs to be prepared by God with grace, in order that he may be raised to things which are above his nature, as was stated above.